CHRISTINE GO

Business
Mum

THREE STEPS TO SUCCESS
IN RUNNING YOUR OWN
BUSINESS AND BEING A MUM

Published by
LID Publishing Limited
The Record Hall, Studio 204,
16-16a Baldwins Gardens,
London EC1N 7RJ, UK

524 Broadway, 11th Floor, Suite 08-120,
New York, NY 10012, US

info@lidpublishing.com
www.lidpublishing.com

A member of:

BPR
Business Publishers Roundtable

www.businesspublishersroundtable.com

Printed in Great Britain by TJ International
ISBN: 978-1-911498-98-8

Cover and page design: Caroline Li

CHRISTINE GOUCHAULT

Business
Mum

THREE STEPS TO SUCCESS IN RUNNING YOUR OWN BUSINESS AND BEING A MUM

LONDON   NEW YORK   SHANGHAI
MADRID   BARCELONA   BOGOTA
MEXICO CITY   MONTERREY   BUENOS AIRES

Contents

STEP 2:
DEVELOP YOUR STRATEGY

STEP 3 :
OPTIMIZE YOUR RESOURCES AND ATTAIN MORE

Preface

A big thanks to all the wonderful, self-employed women who have shared their stories of both adversity and prosperity as sources of inspiration and learning for the rest of us: Anna Bogdanova, Anja Lytzen, Birgitte Feldborg, Birgitte Othel, Camilla Mengers, Jane Ulsøe, Louise Ertman Baunsgaard, Louise Ferslev, Pernille Birkenfeldt and Pia Nissen Tylak.

Thanks to Sif Svejgaard and Charlotte Heje Haase for your feedback and support.

Thanks to Samuel Meijer for finding and correcting my mistakes and for the encouraging words.

And, last but not least, a special thank you to my wonderful husband, Florent, whom I can always count on, and to my lovely children, who always cheer me on.

Introduction

I've written this book for those who want to lead a self-employed life, where there is room for passion and time for family. You've probably discovered that there's a lot to take into account when you start your own business. It can be hard to find good solutions to the challenges you encounter, because many of the answers you come across don't fit with your values and with the life you want to live.

I follow many male entrepreneurs and have learned a lot from their business strategies. At the same time, I've often felt like a more feminine business role model was missing, one which is professional and serious, but also has room for family life.

Men's drive and capacity for action can be inspiring, but I don't want to follow their example when they say that it's their wives and children who pay the price of their hard work. I've never been willing to sacrifice my close relationship with my children or with my husband for the sake of my career. At the same time, I've always wanted to do a lot with my life. So, it's taken me many years and several attempts to try to crack the code for creating a satisfying life as mother and self-employed entrepreneur, where there is a balance between earnings, work and family life. But now that I have succeeded, I'd like to inspire and help you do the same.

Through my own experience and the knowledge I have gained from working with my clients, I want to help you avoid the classic traps entrepreneurs fall into so you can succeed with your business. No matter how committed we may be to work, there are family-friendly ways of being a business owner.

A Big Decision

My work became a barrier when I got pregnant for the third time. I had a good but busy position as a consultant, my work was exciting, and I had a reasonable degree of freedom where I could develop and challenge myself on a regular basis. Unfortunately, much of the work required being present at clients' offices that were far from my home and, in addition, there were often meetings late in the evenings. All of this concerned me, because I felt that I didn't see enough of my two children on a daily basis, and work seemed stressful, with little or no time to myself.

Then it happened – I got pregnant again. The pregnancy was something we wanted, and I was looking forward to being a mother again. But I realized how difficult my daily life would be with a newborn child. I didn't think much about the first scan. My previous pregnancies had been problem-free, so I viewed the scan as more of a formality. My husband hadn't even taken the day off, but as luck would have it, one of his shifts was moved, so he went with me. On our way to see the midwife, we joked about what sex we thought it would be, even though it was still too early to tell. "Does it feel like a boy or like a girl?" my husband asked me.

"Neither," I replied. My abdomen felt sorer than the other times, but I brushed it off. I thought it was probably because I was almost ten years older than the first time I was pregnant.

The midwife smeared my belly thoroughly with gel and applied the scanner to my skin, but raised it quickly again.

"Have you been scanned before?" she asked. I had during the previous pregnancies, but not yet with this one. Her question puzzled me. She put the scanner back on, and at the same time as we saw two round silhouettes on the screen, she noted that it was twins. A sense of joy flowed through my body, and both my husband and I had tears in our eyes. We felt happy when we left the midwife. Although it all felt a bit surreal, the first thoughts I had were about how life would be with a full-time job and four children. Something would have to change radically if we wanted to have enough time to enjoy time with our children – yet we still had to find a solution where we would be able to pay the bills.

Having a family with four small children, being under pressure from all sides and running around frantically on the hamster-wheel of daily life was not the scenario I had envisaged for myself. Though, this was already quite close to the life we were leading with only two children.

I'd long dreamed of becoming self-employed again, and I thought it was now that I should do it, so I could be in control of my own time. This was without a doubt the right decision, although at the time I didn't know what business I would be working in. So, I quit my job during my maternity leave and spent that time thinking about what I should do next, because my business model would have to be more flexible.

It is now two and a half years since I started Mors Business (that's in Danish; Mum's Business in English); a consultancy firm, where I support myself doing what I am passionate about, namely helping, inspiring and motivating other mothers who want to succeed with their business. Here I can make a difference, test my ideas, and continue to develop and challenge myself.

With four children, I certainly have an active life, but it is also a life where most days I can take and pick up all the children, together with my husband. A life where we have time for one another, where I rejoice over all the exciting things I experience and the great people I meet through my work.

It was a big decision to start my own business and become self-employed. This was especially true because my husband also quit his job to become a full-time father, so that we could have more flexibility and spend more time with the kids. We cut down on loads of expenses and swapped the car for a delivery bicycle, allowing me to build up my business without worrying too much about our financial situation.

As always, there have been both ups and downs. There have been projects that didn't go as planned, but also ideas that succeeded far beyond my expectations. I have had my share of doubts and felt unsettled when faced with uncertainty, because I didn't know how everything would turn out in the end. But it has definitely been a more satisfying life – in more ways than one. The pride you take in building something yourself and succeeding, the feeling of being alive when you are on the fringes of your comfort zone, the joy of making a difference and helping others. Having flexibility in your everyday life. And the freedom – the freedom to choose, to be yourself, to work in a way that feels right. It's the most amazing feeling.

Because I have walked the walk, I know it can be done, and through my business I help other women do the same. It's fantastic to witness other people live out their dream of becoming self-employed, and with this book I dearly wish to help you do the same. I would like to help you find your motivation and strength to succeed, give you the tools you need to manage the uncertainty and the obstacles along the way, and show you how to build your business and create a more satisfying daily life in which there's also room for your family.

When you hear of women who are successful, people immediately tend to think "she definitely has either a rich husband or wealthy parents", or "she was born with a great talent that makes everything easier for her" or "she's just plain lucky." People rarely think that she's goal-oriented, courageous and works hard.

Working hard and purposefully for something is seldom looked upon as something positive. At least not when it comes to women. In newspapers and on social media, girls who achieve straight As are targeted and the headlines are often harsh:

"Girls who do well at school crack under pressure and need psychological help"; "If they get good grades, they lack the personality and the right skills to succeed in the labour market"; or "Women's ambitions break them down psychologically." There is a small percentage to whom this does apply, but the vast majority of those who achieve straight As actually manage just fine. We just don't hear that much about the successful straight-A girls because their ambitions, results and passions challenge the unspoken law that states that you must not think you are better than anyone else. But no one speaks negatively about boys who achieve straight As, and fathers with dreams of becoming a CEO are certainly not unheard of.

This is due to an unconscious and conscious gender bias against powerful women and, surprisingly, this bias exists in both men and women in most modern societies. Often, women are punished by our society and in their roles in leadership and management for speaking with confidence. They are perceived far more negatively than men for communicating in the same forceful way and manner as men. Studies on unconscious bias also show that success and likeability are positively correlated for men and negatively correlated for women. There is confirmed research that shows that the more successful a woman is perceived today, the less she is liked. A known case study from Columbia Business School that illustrates this point is the story of Heidi Roizen, a successful Silicon Valley venture capitalist. Two groups of students studied her case. The first group got the study with Heidi's name on it, the other group thought it was about a man named Howard. Both groups rated Howard and Heidi equally competent, however; they liked Howard but not Heidi, and even perceived Heidi as more selfish.

So, it turns out that high-achieving women are neither boring nor anti-social and in fact we can also have it all, if we really want to. These women are merely able to identify their goals and have the guts to pursue them. So can we.

Mothers who are self-employed are the grown-up version of the overachieving girls. These women get to have both: family and the freedom to live out their dreams – and this is something that others feel threatened by. A mother who is successful is viewed almost as a contradiction in terms. It is often assumed that women who are successful on the work front have probably neglected their children, and the negatively charged term 'career mother' is instantly applied.

You are often faced with other people's envy, clichés and prejudices. If there is no one in your circle of friends or family who has chosen the same lifestyle as you, you might have your own prejudices to fight against before you can feel free to let go of some of your own rules and go for the career that you want.

What is a good mother? I believe we all do the best we can with the resources available to us. Depending on our upbringing and values, it can vary, but the most important thing is to be able to look at yourself in the mirror and be satisfied. In Denmark, we have a social system that allows us to both work, have long maternity leave and leave work early. When I lived in France, it was common to work till 6pm – even on Fridays! There wasn't the same emphasis on performing as a mother on the home front. On the other hand, French mothers are more concerned with attending the right school, getting the best education and having a good career. If you've lived in other countries, I'm sure you would have experienced other differences. The important thing is for you to decide what being a good mother means to you. What kind of upbringing and values do you want to give your children? Then simply do the best you can and ignore other people's comments. If you start to get a bad conscience, don't bash yourself for not doing a good enough job. Instead, use your conscience as an indicator that something needs to change, and then do something about it.

In this book, I've chosen to interview a number of self-employed mums with different backgrounds, types of businesses and experiences, so you have different role models to choose from. Hopefully, you will relate to one of their stories. They all demonstrate that you can have time for your family while building your business, and that there are truly a great number of ways you can create a satisfying life.

You will soon begin to realize that although each of these women chose different paths and did not have the same premises when starting their own business, they all have a common denominator when it comes to mindset, courage, vigour and perseverance. Your education, your relationship status or your age do not, alone, determine your success. It's all about taking your circumstances and making the best out of them. Where there is a will, there is certainly a way, and with this book I hope to inspire you to follow your heart and choose your own path.

The Many Detours

Mors Business is not my first company. It has taken me several attempts and many detours to get to where I am today. My journey in becoming self-employed began when, at the age of 25, I started a recruiting agency in Paris, together with a partner.

It all started as a love story. I went to Paris to be with the man I loved and we got married. The most obvious next step was to complete my studies in France, as I already knew French, and my husband did not yet speak Danish. I got an MA in communication, and next I needed to get a trainee position. I found a position in a small entrepreneurial firm that mediated job advertising between companies and newspapers. Then, in 2005, the market switched from placing job ads in newspapers to online job ads, which made it difficult for the mediators to earn the kind of money they were earning before. The advent of online ads meant that the cost of an ad was a tenth of what it was previously.

Customers began ask for help with recruitment instead, as at the time they received as many as 300 applications and many calls for each listed position. I had a good working relationship with my employer, and we started a recruiting agency. Neither of us had a background in human resources, but we invested in a private recruitment course, got certified in personality tests, and then we were on our way.

At the time, I didn't doubt for a second that it was the right thing for me. I loved my job, I was having fun, and I felt challenged in a positive and growth-oriented way. I was even earning a living. But, I was working a lot, which became a problem when I had children and wanted to spend time with them. So, I made the tough decision to sell my share of the business and move to Denmark, where our society is friendlier towards families with small children.

It was hard to let go of my job and business; it was like a third child for me. However, this decision turned out to be the right one for our family, and I am very grateful for all the time I had and still have with my children, so I definitely have no regrets.

I was always sure that I would start another business. I'm an entrepreneur by nature, and I enjoy the freedom and the responsibility that comes with it. However, the financial crisis hit when we had just moved back to Denmark in 2008, and I had to get a job to pay the bills. It felt as if I had to compromise myself and my identity. On the outside, it might have looked good, because I have had a number of good consulting jobs, but I felt as if I had to ignore an important part of who I am.

It was not the right time to start a new business then, so I focused on amassing experience and skills that could equip me to create a good business at a later date. I chose jobs where I could develop my sales skills and create a network. I worked on myself and took coaching courses, as well as courses on marketing and performance. These were all skills and knowledge I knew I'd be able to use in my own company someday. I have tried various jobs and learned from them all to get to the business I have today, and it's still evolving, as I evolve as a person.

As I got to know the Danish market better, expanded my professional network and got my coach certifications, I felt ready to be my own boss again. I started two businesses. First with a group of consultants, where we almost immediately realized the concept wouldn't work; then later with a friend, but after six months she and I had to face the fact that we were too different – and then we chose to shut down the company. Both times, it felt like being punched in the stomach, because I had to let go of my dream and start all over again.

And why am I telling you all this?

Well, because seen from the outside, it could appear as if I have had two good businesses: one in Paris that I sold, and the one I have now, which is correct, of course.

But there were also ten years where I had other jobs and tried lots of things. It hasn't been linear and clear-cut from the beginning. The chance of your business being that way is not that big, either. There are many things you learn throughout your career. Things you can read about but not quite understand, because some things must be experienced first-hand, not just read about. Just like when you were young and you read about falling in love, having children or getting married, and understood it on an intellectual level, only to learn later that reality is quite different when you experience things for yourself.

From a business point of view, I'd rather have continued with my business in Paris. My partner did, and today he has eight employees and a revenue of over £4 million per year. I had a lot of detours throughout my career and therefore, I don't have that kind of revenue with my firm – far from it. But for me, the fundamental factor has always been to have time for my family.

Whether or not I reach £4 million annual revenue is not crucial. My point is that it takes time to build up a business, and there's no straight path. The most important thing is knowing what your goal is, and that you do what is right for you, so you can enjoy the journey and have time for those you love while building your business.

Know that you're not a failure if you don't succeed at once. If you've never been self-employed before, you can't possibly know what it is like. Sometimes it takes more and something different from what you expect, and you won't find out till you've started. As the entrepreneur and life-coach Tony Robbins says: "Stay committed to your decisions, but stay flexible in your approach." If your dream is to be able to live through self-employment, go for it and don't give up, but be open to there being many ways you can succeed with the dream, and to the fact that some paths will only reveal themselves along the journey.

Luckily, you don't have to spend as much time as I did to create a good life as a self-employed mother. In this book, I'm sharing with you the best tools and methods I have developed in order to succeed. These are the tools I used to build up Mors Business, and the ones I teach my clients to help them reach their goals.

In this book, the tools have been divided into three steps to make them easier to follow.

STEP 1

Find Your Drive and Let Go of Your Brakes

Find Your Drive

What motivates you to succeed in being self-employed? What gives you the enthusiasm and the energy to keep going, without knowing when and if you will succeed?

For me there are two things: the stick and the carrot. The stick represents what I want to avoid and my worst-case scenario – which is a life bound to a pay cheque. A life where others rule over my time and restrict my ideas and my room to manoeuvre without really appreciating who I am as a person; and more importantly, stopping me from developing my potential and becoming who I want to be.

The carrot, which represents what drives and motivates me, has three components:

- the freedom to choose and try out new ideas and challenge my limits;
- the joy of doing what I am passionate about, to be able to make a greater difference and help more people;
- all the inspiring people I meet in the entrepreneurial community.

My longing for freedom is clearly bigger than my need for financial security, though it can be nerve-wracking not knowing how much I am going to earn when I am self-employed.

Although the stick can be an effective tool to get you to act and adversity can make you strong, it's the carrot you have to get hold of to thrive in the long run. Your business must be based on desire, not fear.

Life as a self-employed individual is often lived on the edge of your comfort zone. It puts you on an emotional roller-coaster with ups and downs, where sometimes you will go through the whole emotional spectrum of anger, joy, sadness, fear and hope in one day. You need to have a firm hold on your motivations to stick to the things that keep your business moving forward. Otherwise you'll spend your precious time working on the safe side with formalities that have to be completed at some point, but which ultimately don't have that much influence on whether or not you'll succeed.

Most people experience a 'high' and feel energized when they first start their own business, and they run around with butterflies in their stomach. It's great and exciting, but everyday life quickly catches up with you. That can be both a good and a bad thing. Being self-employed is a lifestyle, and that's why it has to fit around you and the life you want to lead.

A good strategy or plan of action is important for you to reach your goals, but it's even more important that you start by working on yourself, since it's you who has to implement the plan, keep your motivation alive and make the right decisions. It takes perseverance, courage, willpower and strength to succeed. In this chapter, we'll look at the basic things that are critical in how your business and your life as a self-employed person turn out, namely:

- What drives you
- What can stop you

You will learn some very powerful and practical exercises. For that reason, you should set aside time to work on yourself, your business and your vision. This is also the way you create success: by being conscious, making choices and taking action.

Create a Sustainable Lifestyle

The first thing you need to think about is where you want your business and your life to take you. Then you can make the right decisions to get there. If you don't have a clear idea of what you want, you can easily choose solutions that feel right in the moment, but serve no wider purpose and might even hurt your business.

Vision exercises are some of the most effective tools I've come across in identifying the important things in life. You might have tried it already and think that you know yourself well enough and what you want. Even so, I recommend that you complete one or more of the exercises in this chapter; they will help you to manage the doubts that may crop up as you develop your business.

Put simply, your vision is the image of how you want your future to be. What will you be doing? Where will you be? Who will you be with? And how will you feel about being you? A good vision is one that motivates you, that makes you want to act upon your dreams and to find solutions to the challenges you might come across. It's a kind of guiding star that inspires, guides and helps you when you have to make tough decisions.

It's not hard to act upon the vision when you're convinced of what you want and why. As a consequence, you might have to exclude some people from your life or make other drastic changes to create the life you've envisioned. If you haven't 'listened' to yourself for a long time, it might be challenging when you discover how much you have to change in order to get the life you want.

If your present life is very far from what you want it to be, it can require a number of changes and at times make you feel afraid and uncertain. There will most likely be 'off days' as you start choosing what's important for you, and others can react negatively to it. It's difficult and uncomfortable in the beginning, but you will find that it is worth it in the end, and the quality of your life will improve immensely.

If you've worked on your vision before, you may discover that it has changed over time. This is because you have evolved since you made it. For that reason, it's also a good idea to repeat these exercises and ask yourself these questions again once some time has passed and you've reached the first milestones with your business.

Vision Exercise Number 1 – Collecting the Clues

This first exercise helps you determine what you want from your life and your business.

Start by reading each question and write down all the answers that come to you.

If you stop dead in your tracks after a couple of words, you can ask yourself: "What else do I want?" "What else could it be?" By asking yourself open questions like these, you encourage your brain to keep on searching for answers when it has ground to a halt. You can also use the question: "What might be one thing that ... ?"

Right now, it's about brainstorming and opening up for ideas. You can always sort your ideas out later.

- If you couldn't fail, and success was assured, what would you do with your business?
- If you had enough money, what would you want to do?
- What does your ideal work week look like?
- What are you doing?
- Which work tasks energize you?

- Which work tasks would you rather avoid?
- Who (which clients) do you want to help?
- What would you like your clients to say about you?
- What feelings do you have when you're working?
- If someone wrote an article about you, what would it say?
- Where do you want to live?
- What do you do when you're not working?
- Who do you want to be with when you're working – and in your spare time?

One of our greatest needs as human beings is contributing and giving in order to feel that we make a difference. This gives our actions meaning and can help us overcome adversity, because we can see a greater purpose in what we do. Some of you may say that it's your calling, your 'why', your reason for being. When you're aware of how you want to contribute and why, it will make it easier for you to develop your business. Your 'why' is a part of the foundation you stand on to create the life you dream of.

- Who do you want to help?
- What kind of a difference do you want to make?
- What do you want to contribute?

Now take your answers and rewrite them in the present.

Don't be afraid of sounding foolish. It's okay to dream and think big. If the vision doesn't give you butterflies, then keep working on it. It only works correctly if it's something you really believe in doing.

Work with your vision until you feel it inspires you and makes you happy. It should describe your dream scenario. How long it turns out to be is entirely up to you. If you're not too fond of writing, you can make a collage or a vision board instead, with pictures that symbolize your vision. The most important thing is that it inspires and motivates you.

The next exercises will help you develop your vision and see it from other angles.

Vision Exercise Number 2 – The Measuring Tape

Essentially this exercise results in another way of thinking about your life. Insert your answers into your vision.

You can use a measuring tape or make one out of a long piece of paper, marking on it numbers starting from 1 through to 100.

1. Cut the measuring tape at your present age.
   > Look at it and think of what you've experienced.
   > When did something big happen that changed your life?
   > How does it feel to look at – and think about?

2. Cut the measuring tape at the age you think you'll reach.
   > Look at the years that are left of your life.
   > What experiences do you want to put into them?
   > What feelings do you want to put into them?
   > How does it feel to look at – and think about?

When you look at the measuring tape, you'll get new insights that will help you decide what you want for yourself in the future. It gives a more personal perspective than the first exercise, which is more focused on your business and working life.

Vision Exercise Number 3 – Your Own Funeral

This is a powerful exercise and will put you in touch with many of your feelings. Start by closing your eyes; the more you close your eyes and feel before you answer, the better the exercise will work. If you can get a person you trust to ask you the questions, it's even better.

It's best to do this exercise when you're up to it and it's peaceful around you. You may find that it helps to have a friend close by so that you have someone to talk to afterwards.

Imagine that you're going to die in three years' time:
- What do you want to say to your husband/significant other/partner before you die?
- What do you want to say to your child/children before you die?
- What do you want to say to your friends and closest family before you die?

Now, imagine that you could observe your own funeral:
- What do you want your husband/significant other/ partner to say about you?
- What do you want your child/children to say about you?
- What do you want your friends and closest family to say about you?

Insert your answers in your vision; these will become strong and motivational factors for you.

When you've created your vision (using any one or all three of these exercises), the next step is to turn it into reality.

1. Start by writing down what has to happen in order for the vision to become a reality. Let your answers be 'goals'.
2. After that, write down sub-goals. What do you have to do, step by step, to reach your goals? This book will help you make a plan, so you don't have to have everything in place right now.
3. Add dates. If the dream doesn't make its way to the calendar, it will remain a dream.
4. If possible, find a person you can be accountable to. Every month show this person how far you've come and evaluate this in relation to your goals and sub-goals.
5. Imagine for a couple of minutes every day how it feels when your vision starts to become a reality. How does it feel to know that you are working towards it every day?

When you anchor that feeling in your body every day by imagining where you're heading, you automatically make it easier for yourself to stay focused and make the right decisions to turn your vision into reality. In any business, an entrepreneur will find they have to make a great number of decisions based on what feels right or wrong. This gives a powerful drive and direction to steer your business in the right direction.

Listen to Your Intuition

Creating a compelling vision is simple. Following it is harder. One of the greatest challenges is daring to listen to your intuition and following your heart when you make decisions in your business. It might seem easy when doing the vision exercises, but it's all put to the test when you face adversity or have to make some tough decisions in everyday life. It's not enough to have sufficient trust in yourself, take the plunge and start your business; you also have to be true to yourself afterwards in everything you do.

Louise Ertman Baunsgaard is a woman that successfully followed her heart and her gut feeling and built a well-functioning business. She was 27 when in 2003 she opened her first takeaway restaurant, Letz Sushi. The restaurant has performed well from the start, thanks to her intuition and a great deal of hard work. It all started with two months' leave of absence when she visited Australia and got inspired by the way the sushi restaurants in Sydney sold creative sushi of high quality at reasonable prices.

"The company I worked for had been sold and my colleagues and I were waiting to get dismissed. I didn't know

29

how to make sushi, but I was good at coming up with new concepts and marketing.

"I had £40,000 of equity in my apartment, so I got a loan to start with. I didn't worry about losing my investment. I was in my twenties and had no kids, so I thought I could always earn it back," Louise says.

"I had to hire a chef from the start to make the sushi and, in the beginning, I relied on friends to work at the counter. The takeaway restaurant was open every day from 12 to 9pm – when you have customers every day you earn money, so I never had any problems paying myself. My company grew organically, so I didn't look for investors in the beginning, like many start-ups do nowadays."

Louise had jumped right into an industry in which she had no professional experience.

"Many people around me thought I was crazy to start a sushi restaurant. They said sushi was a passing trend that would end soon, that I should keep my good job in the IT business. But I didn't care. You can't listen to everybody; it confuses and influences you to doubt yourself. Time alone to think and feel what you really want is crucial, especially when your company is growing," Louise insists.

"I learned how to be efficient and get many things done in a short amount of time. I focused and prioritized doing one thing at a time, and I made fast decisions. I think the fast decisions made me survive. I feel it in my gut. Especially in the beginning, I'd ask myself, what feels right, right here and now? And then I acted on it."

It paid well for Louise to follow her intuition. "A year later, when I opened my second restaurant, I felt that I was skilled at what I was doing. It also made me feel good that I was free to decide how to spend my own time and have a good life. I never had a particular strategy for my business, but have always prioritized location. I made sure to let the business grow organically, so I never hired more people or grew the business faster than I could handle," Louise explains.

In 2013, Louise merged with another sushi chain and the restaurants from the other chain were turned into the Letz Sushi concept. At the same time, she sold 50% of her company to get capital to take her business to the next level.

"Scaling came naturally, because they found me. At that point, I had seven restaurants and just my own money. If I wanted to grow I needed to get not just money, but more knowledge inside the company and have someone to help make the strategic decisions. It was nice to get someone on board, but it also meant working really closely together and letting go of some of my freedom. I think most people tend to forget that, when they 'just' want someone to invest money in their business. With the money comes obligations and the results have to follow."

Her business continued to grow and after 14 years she owned 16 restaurants, had more than 150 employees and a turnover of approximately £6 million a year. She sold the company in the summer of 2017 and is now one of the few female business angels in Denmark who actively invests in start-ups and inspires women to start their own businesses.

Find Your Strengths as an Entrepreneur

Now that you're your own boss, organize your work so you feel like sticking to it. No one becomes a success overnight. It takes time and perseverance to succeed. When in the midst of my work, as much as I enjoy spending time with family, I feel that I begrudge weekends and look forward to Mondays. There are lots of stops you can pull out towards creating a wonderful work-life balance for yourself, which I will show you in this chapter. It doesn't mean everything is peachy, but if you're not motivated, it's hard to stick around for the long haul and get your business going. The best thing is to create a daily routine where tasks feel enjoyable, so you can get through them and, in time, create a successful business.

However, it is easy to transfer bad habits from previous jobs. I'm sure you know the feeling of having a job that isn't quite you, either because the work tasks are boring, the boss is unpleasant, work hours are too rigid, your colleagues gossip about everyone, or something else entirely different. It's draining and demoralizing in the long run, and if you don't make conscious decisions that feed you positive energy, these can affect you, even as an entrepreneur. For example, if you are easily distracted during working hours, why not go for a long walk and get some fresh air and inspiration?

By organizing your work in a way that feels good to you, a lot of energy and creativity to develop yourself and your business will be released. For example, one of my strengths is my holistic approach to work and being good at seeing the bigger picture, breaking down complex tasks into concrete plans that my clients can follow. On the downside, I'm not too concerned with details. So, I am more than happy to pay someone to proofread my written work.

Exercise: Finding Your Strengths

If you've had a personal profile analysis (or a personality test), you may already know your strengths. By carrying out this exercise, you'll get an overview of your dominant behaviours and strengths in a work context. These nine areas are inspired by Master Danmark's MPA personality profile analysis that I've used for a number of years in my work. Read through the list, and select the sentence under each question that you relate to. You'll get the best result if you answer quickly and follow your intuition and don't give it too much thought. If you feel torn between two sentences, choose the statement where you really recognize your own behaviour.

1. How do you work with goals and results?

A. I'm mostly process-oriented, and I prefer long time deadlines and to focus on quality.

B. I'm mostly results-oriented and competitive, and prefer focusing on goals, sub-goals and quantity.

2. How do you seek influence?

A. I mostly listen, and I rarely express my opinions. I'm good at adapting in a group.

B. I often take the lead, successfully get my viewpoints across and seek great influence.

3. How do you prioritize tasks and time?

A. I prefer time to immerse myself in things and having only a few tasks.

B. I prefer many tasks and great variety.

4. What is your need for social contact?

A. I prefer working alone or in small groups.

B. I enjoy being seen, talking to many people and creating new relationships.

5. How do you show your feelings at work?

A. I rarely show my feelings. I'm rational, focused on the task at hand and seem unconcerned.

B. I often show my feelings, I worry, and am easily influenced by moods and situations.

6. How do you handle conflict?

A. I often speak my mind. I say no, I am direct and face conflicts head-on.

B. I'm mostly forthcoming and trusting. I say yes to most things and avoid conflicts.

7. What's your approach to your work tasks?
A. I'm mostly focused on the details. I am thorough and enjoy routine work.
B. I can maintain an overview. I focus on the whole picture, I prefer variation and have no problem delegating.

8. How do you make decisions?
A. I ponder intensely over things and have long decision-making processes.
B. I mostly make quick decisions. I'm spontaneous, I take chances, and I act quickly upon my thoughts.

9. How creative and innovative are you?
A. I'm mostly practical and specific, and I like having guidelines.
B. I prefer being theoretical and abstract, and I focus on alternative options and new ideas.

After you've chosen the nine behavioural traits that best describe you, think of specific situations where you've used each of these qualities. A specific situation could be being presented with a new opportunity and immediately saying "yes." If in doubt, you can ask someone who knows you well. Our nearest and dearest can always recognize our typical behaviours and strengths.

Your Greatest Strength Is Often Your Greatest Weakness

It can be a bit tricky working with strengths and weaknesses, as your greatest strength can often be your greatest weakness. The situation you're in determines the character trait relevant to you. For example, I'm very optimistic, I'm good at finding solutions and am not afraid of jumping head first into something new; these are generally considered as strengths. On the downside, my optimism means I'm often unaware of what can go wrong, and I don't always prepare well enough. Among other things, that meant the first time I was going to market a course I started my sales campaign far too late, and I didn't communicate enough because I expected the participants were sure to buy a ticket for my course. The outcome was that no one showed up, and I had to start from scratch again.

It's important to know your strengths and weaknesses. Knowing them means that you can take them into consideration and get help where necessary. For example, showing empathy is a strength when listening to clients and understanding their needs; it helps you offer products or services they need. On the other hand, empathy might make you forget to listen to yourself and take your own needs seriously.

Exercise: Take your five greatest strengths into consideration and find examples of situations where they can be weaknesses.

The advantage of knowing when your strengths can be weaknesses is that you can use this knowledge to steer clear of trouble. Now that I'm aware of how my optimism can misguide me, I often talk to someone more realistic or pessimistic to get a perspective of what can go wrong and take this into account when I make new plans for the future.

Create Situations That Engage Your Strengths

When you're aware of your strengths, you can make maximum use of them, and even create situations where weaknesses support you. I once had a client who was very impatient and easily lost concentration – her thoughts skipped from one idea to the other. She wanted to publish a book, and she already had a contract with a publishing house, but she just couldn't pull herself together to sit down and write, even though she was passionate about the subject matter. She wondered if she should avoid the distractions at home by taking a few days out to force herself to work. She also had to complete her tax returns, which she was already late in delivering. Again, the distractions piled up, and she ended up doing all kinds of other things. On the other hand, she had a huge drive when she was doing something she enjoyed. Therefore, we looked for patterns in her work and looked into changing her work procedures accordingly. She was working on a total of four projects, and we split them up so she'd work 15 minutes at a time on each and then switch. By allowing herself to work in small portions, and switching among the four projects, she found her spark and got a lot more work done.

Now it no longer felt like a chore, and in the first week she finished the last chapters of her book and completed her accounts, so both could be sent off.

For some, it may be a nightmare working this way, and perhaps you prefer to go into depth with what you're working on, for many hours or days at a time. The point is, you have to find a way of working that suits you, and forget about all the rules or what you did in your previous workplace.

Likewise, just as strengths can be weaknesses, your weaknesses can also be strengths in certain situations. Very few care to be called selfish, but it can be a huge help when you have to make decisions for yourself and for your business. As I mentioned earlier, my lack of sense for details means I'm very decisive and I move quickly and get results. For a long time, my homepage only had a badly taken selfie photo and a picture of my eBook. A year passed before I had professional pictures taken. Had I had a sense for details, I would have insisted on having all website collateral ready, and a good homepage from the beginning. But instead, I chose to focus on writing relevant content to engage with my audience, and as a result, I got over 1,700 readers for my newsletters and lots of clients before better photos were added. There is no reason to bash your head with your weaknesses, because if you're aware of it, there's always a strength hidden in them that can help you with your business.

Exercise: Try looking at your three key weaknesses and find examples of situations where they have played as strengths.

Your Quirks Are Your Strengths

I often feel that some people within the self-employed community have a somewhat limited idea of how we should act professionally. That like everybody else, we maintain a certain appearance. The type of appearance depends on the working environment of the business. Maybe you're used to having to be very formal, but you would, in fact, rather be more spontaneous and natural.

For a long time, I was under the illusion that I had to be like everybody else to fit in. When I had my own business in Paris, I was a young, woman in my mid-20s. My clients were male business owners in their 40s and 50s. At an unconscious level, I felt I wasn't good enough and that I should be something more. To make up for my youth, my gender and my nationality – which I felt put me in a weaker position – I dressed in grey and formal attire, so hopefully no one would notice. My business partner was a man 12 years my senior. He had the same firm convictions as I did. So, when we were visiting clients he always did the talking, and I would come across as his assistant rather than his partner. At the time, I didn't think much of it, because business was good, and for the most part, we had fun together.

Unfortunately, I brought my conviction with me to Denmark, and when I was about to start a business again, I was immediately on the lookout for a partner – precisely because I didn't feel confident or good enough alone. First, I tried to establish a cooperation with three consultants who were about 60 years old; I felt honoured that they would even consider a venture with someone as young as myself. I let go of it quickly, though, because the prospects of real income based on their concepts were very long term. After some years, I tried again. This time, with a girlfriend 20 years my senior. She had experience in leadership, which I didn't have, and I felt I needed her to appear credible to sell consultant services to managers. Somehow, my studies and my business experience were not enough, in my own eyes. To my surprise, and against my expectations, it turned out that I had no trouble selling myself as a consultant, without anyone making comments on my lack of leadership experience. After six months, my cooperation with her ended because we were too different. But I still hadn't learned my lesson. I went on and accepted a job as a consultant where I did my very best to hide the fact that I had young children, and instead I wanted to show that I was one of the guys.

It was only when I became pregnant with twins and had to quit my job that I started thinking that things could and should be different. I didn't want to start a new business where I felt I had to apologize for who I am, or for the life I have. Hence, the idea for Mors Business. I wanted to start a business where it was a strength being the mother of four. I wanted more than just to be free to dispose of my time; I also wanted to be free to be myself.

Today, having spoken to numerous clients, I realized that, in fact, this kind of thinking is more common than I had thought. I wasn't alone in thinking this way and many of us carry these kinds of limiting convictions and believe that we should be someone other than ourselves. The funny thing is, it's the total opposite. It's 20 times easier to stick out from the competition and get a handful of clients you really enjoy working with when you are comfortable being yourself and you acknowledge your quirks. People buy from people, and we're more attracted to those who share the same values/quirks and dare to be honest about who they are. It doesn't mean you have to become a lifestyle blogger and turn your soul inside out; you just need to be true to yourself.

Perhaps you don't feel too young, but it's not a question of age. I myself have interviewed a number of successful self-employed mothers, who show that you can succeed, no matter how restrictive your story is. Mette Weber only started her online business at the age of 60 – without having any technical prerequisites. Michelle Hviid succeeded in her business, despite being a single mother of two children and her courageous way of handling her brain tumour made her even more popular. Despite a tough childhood and being from an ethnic minority, Soulaima Gourani has fought her way up and become a recognized international business advisor.

By looking at learnings and strengths in your story, you can stand even taller as a self-employed businesswoman. There are bound to be many other businesses that offer the same service or product as yours does, but there is only one of you, with exactly your experience, your education, your values and your personality.

Exercise: Practice telling or writing your story down.
- What are your 'quirks'?
- What interests you?
- Which decisions have you made that character-ize you?
- What have you done that's 'different'?
- And how can you use that in regards to your business?

From Employee to Self-Employed

A good example of this is Camilla Mengers and her husband, Michael. They both have the equivalent of a bachelor's degree in social education and worked with children in preschool education and share a common interest in recycled goods and visiting flea markets. They don't exactly resemble the typical café owners in trendy Hornbæk, where most of North Zealand gathers in the summer. They come from a world where the focus is more on relationships than on money. They had neither enough starting capital, nor did they earn enough to get a bank loan, and they'd never made a business plan before.

When visiting a flea market, they got a taste for earning money of their own, and the dream of doing something where they bought and resold goods started to grow on them. They wanted to create a place where customers could stay a bit longer, with tasty coffee and homemade baked goods. A place with good service, where everyone felt welcome. They wanted to go back to the basics. They felt that good personalized service is becoming increasingly rare, as machines are providing services more and more, in banks and libraries, for example. They toyed with the idea, even before having children while they were living in Copenhagen. They moved to Hornbæk with their daughter Alberte, and after their son Mingus was born, they started looking for a place, that could house both a café and their home. Michael earned less, as he only worked 27 hours a week, since it was important for them that one of them spent extra time with the children. As a result, they didn't have much money which meant that they missed out on many possibilities because they couldn't secure a loan either. So they shelved the idea.

But the dream kept tugging at them, so when a house on the main street in Hornbæk went up for sale, they chose to make their move. The house was large enough for their family to live in and had space for a café downstairs. This was perfect; they'd always be home and close to the children, even when they were working. They were lucky enough to be able to borrow money from a friend for the payment until they were able to sell their own house.

"We had all the furnishings we'd bought at flea markets over the years," Camilla says. "Michael quit his job a month before we opened the café, and he was busy, because of all the work that had to be done before we moved in. With help from an architect, we prioritized the work required, which turned into a long checklist for Michael."

In June 2015, they opened Albi's Kaffebar. The plan was that Camilla would take three months leave to help out in the summer and maybe start full-time when the café made a profit. After just a month, they found that they were so busy that Michael declared: "Camilla, you're never going back," and it ended with her boss cycling over to get her resignation because she didn't have time to leave the café to go and hand it in.

Camilla and Michael found and developed an idea that the locals had wanted. An informal and cosy place where you meet over a cup of coffee with homemade baked goods. Their relationship skills as teachers proved to be ideal in customer service, and they achieved the personalized and cosy feeling they had wanted to provide. Being in the cafe actually feels like being in someone's lounge. The atmosphere is relaxed, and the furniture is all recycled, and available for sale, which is part of the concept.

Flea market sales are still a hobby, and they buy things in their spare time or on eBay, so things like lamps, books, tables and different decorations are always being added to the decor.

As for the food, Camilla makes everything herself – except for the chocolate-covered marshmallow puffs. In the beginning, there was one muffin sort, the cake of the day and buns, but this has expanded, as there was a demand for gluten-free pastries. Now there are also gluten-free cakes made with dates and Greek salad with gluten-free crispbread. Every now and then, there are cookies and homemade ice cream in muffin forms. They want to avoid throwing away food, so if you come late in the afternoon, the cakes might be sold out. When there are muffins left over, Camilla makes rumballs, which are round confectionary chocolate cakes with rum flavor covered with chocolate sprinkle. They are now so sought after that cyclists pedal the 25 miles from Copenhagen to enjoy them.

They had made a business plan themselves before starting, but it was only guesswork as to what they would sell, and they were terribly wrong. Luckily they erred in the right direction, because they ended up doing much better than expected. For example, they started small, with a little coffee machine, and invested in a larger and more expensive model the following year.

"We thought a lot, and had many sleepless nights before starting," Camilla says. "So much had to come together.

We use an external accountant, because that's not our strong suit. We'd taken all the practical things into consideration, and we knew that it could work because we only had to pay rent for one place, and we had no staff expenses. I bake everything myself, which gives a bigger profit margin. We made the business plan based on a model we found online, and projected a low turnover initially. We were already used to Michael not earning that much, and we've never been the frivolous types. Some people think it's smart being self-employed, because one can deduct so much in taxes, but one needs to have money to spend before one can deduct it again, so we're not thinking much about that. It's cool opening up a place and living in it at the same time, because our dream had to function alongside the children. Of course, it's been tough with the rejections and the disappointment of the dreams that didn't amount to anything, but then, when you find the right thing, you know why it didn't work the other times. But now, we've found a great house, where there's also a good, private garden and a flat. It's easier now when the children are ill, because we're there and don't have to flip a coin to find out who'll stay home. Now, I always advise others to take a leap of faith and follow their dreams, but also that they must expect to be real about it and work hard. Some people have the idea that we're just having a cosy time at the café, and on a slow day we might sit back and enjoy a cup of coffee out in the sun, but there's an incredible amount of preparatory work involved with cleaning and making food."

Camilla loves the contact with people in the café. "We know everybody who drops in. There are many locals, different types of people, and people of all ages – all the way from ten-year-olds to elderly retirees. Everyone has been very positive towards the concept. The close relationship we have with them allows us to close our doors once in a while and have a day off."

They had to learn how to be visible online. Camilla says: "We bought an iPad, and every day I posted photos of the cake of the day and possible events on Facebook and Instagram. It worked, and attracted more people. It was our daughter Alberte who taught us that, and an acquaintance who works in marketing created our business profile. It works, because we have around 2,200 followers on Facebook and 400 on Instagram, and a Google account where people are so kind and leave us great reviews."

It's not always praise you get on the net, but the café's customers are very loyal. Their behaviour bears witness to the fact that you can come a long way with clear values and a focus on relationships, and without a big business plan to start with.

"A lady posted a negative comment on Facebook once, something along the lines of: 'What's this pollution on the main street? Is the cake recycled too?' and called us losers. In the course of a couple of hours, she got over 200 responses from people in our defence. It's truly wonderful that people like us, and give us so much support. That's also what keeps us going: the positive feedback and the fact that our customers appreciate us," Camilla says.

Let Go of Your Brakes

Succeeding with your business has a lot to do with your mindset. The more you can focus on what you want, where you want to get to, what you have to do to get there and then act upon that, the more likely you are to succeed. What often trips up many self-employed people, myself included, is allowing doubt to fill your mind and putting a brake on actions. Typically, that happens when things don't go as expected. Instead of saying "never mind," learning from the experience and moving on, we stop and start looking at what other people do – especially on social media. We allow ourselves to be distracted by our surroundings and lose focus as a result. Suddenly, we spend a lot of time being insecure, our energy dwindles, and it becomes hard to take action. From being proactive and positive, we do a 180-degree turn, where everything feels like an uphill battle. It's particularly hard when you get mentally sidetracked as a self-employed entrepreneur, and it can be hard yanking yourself up.

"Oh, no! What have I got myself into?" Jane Ulsøe thought like this when the reality of being self-employed caught up with her after having been in business for only a couple of months. In 2014, Jane started the company Canvas Planner with her younger sister, Nanna. It is a tech firm that provides online software for visual project management. Jane followed her sister into the business gradually, and only joined full time in 2016. In 2017, they were nominated for the Danish Entrepreneur Prize in the Young Stars category. Although they were doing well, there had been many ups and downs along the way. Compared with her old job – where she'd been for nine years – in her new business she was familiar with the work, she could work from home, and she had a good deal of freedom to be with her children.

"Well, financially I like to stay on the safe side and at the time I had a house, a car, two children and many fixed expenses. So, even when the bank gave me the green light, and knowing that my husband has a good income, it was still nerve-wracking not having a fixed income. But in 2016 we started getting clients, and I felt that I should either be in it for the long run or let it go. I thought about it for a long time and made the final decision over the summer. But, I still found the financial aspect challenging – being without a fixed income hit me hard. During the day, I did fairly well, but then the worries came over me at night. I thought you only got stressed from working too much, but I didn't get enough sleep, and had a stress reaction to the uncertainty," Jane said.

Jane got help from a good friend who is a psychologist, who helped her put her feelings into perspective.

"My friend explained to me it's a 'primeval thing' that makes me want to put things into systems and fix them. Her advice was to give it time, and to not think about solutions for a period of six months. Instead, I should turn off my thoughts, and not do or read about things that could get me worried. Therefore, I read stories from the 19th century that have nothing to do with my reality, and I chose not to follow the news. This instantly helped me, I was fine again, and I have since found it relatively easy to tackle tough periods using this advice. It's also wonderful being in business with my sister; as a pair, we are able to use each other as sounding boards for our ideas."

"When starting off a business, you have to be ready for the long haul. In tech, many talk about the time when one's business soars, but only few experience that. Instead, I believe that apart from a good idea, it's thoroughness, hard work and drive that make a difference. You have to be prepared for the days being fraught with extreme ups and downs. I have experienced more fluctuations in one day than there were in weeks when I was an employee. That said, it's great to experience the big victories and, really, also the punches. You learn a lot about yourself and your business, and you certainly never get bored."

"Being self-employed also makes you more public and visible. You're naturally very connected to your brand or product when you're at events, and that's taken some getting used to," Jane says. At times, she sees her LinkedIn network growing by 50 people a week.

Despite the emotional ups and downs, Jane doesn't doubt for a moment that it's all worth it. "Starting from scratch and having a business has been a fantastic experience. It's a joy going out to businesses and experiencing their enthusiasm for our product. I feel we are making a difference for our clients. There's a huge freedom associated with being self-employed. It's a great gift being able to manage your own time, and work from home the days it makes sense. It's good having that much influence and being able to turn your work volume up and down."

Three Tools to Handle Fear and Insecurity

When insecure, the solution is – for those who know it, like Jane – quite simple. You must keep on doing what you feel a passion for and stick to your plan. You might not be where you wish to be at the moment, but one thing's for sure: you'll get there faster if you keep on taking action rather than if you do nothing. Of course, it's easier said than done. That's why I'm giving you some tools to keep you on track, so you don't get distracted by fear and insecurity.

It might be helpful to keep in mind that nature has programmed our bodies to react quickly when we're exposed to danger. It's a survival mechanism that ensures we don't get eaten by predators, or that we move away before being run down in traffic. Our spontaneous reactions have protected us through the ages, but they aren't always appropriate in our modern society.

Becoming self-employed is, for many people, an uncertain process: You try something new, you stake your economic security for a while, and prepare yourself to being very vulnerable in many ways. This sets off danger signals in our bodies, and fear rears its ugly head. Negative experiences take up more space than the positive ones.

Depending on which studies you may have read, it takes between two to ten times more positive feedback to make up for one piece of negative feedback. In other words, your fear will be activated more frequently while you develop your business. Your body's spontaneous strategy will typically be fight, flight or freeze, which are seldom the best solutions to the challenge you might be faced with.

I have collected three effective and reasonably quick tools to steer your mindset back on track, back to a positive one. You can use these based on what lies behind your concerns.

1. THE SUCCESS DIARY

One of the things you can do to handle this type of situation is to start keeping a diary, or creating a document or file. Here you should write down all your success stories, big and small, and gather positive feedback from clients, former colleagues, friends and family. Writing and the reading these uplifting pieces will remind you that you're good enough, competent, appreciated, can do it and so on. This has a powerful and quick impact when you are troubled by doubt or fear. The more positively you can look at a situation, the better. It sounds trivial, but if you look at it every day, you'll end up having a good, solid belief that you will succeed.

2. YOUR STATE OF STRENGTH

Another exercise you can do is to find your own state of strength. Your state of strength is the way you are when you have a surplus of energy and are in balance.

Think of a situation where you feel strong, have a surplus of energy and are in balance. Try to describe how you feel in that situation. How does it feel? What are you thinking? What do you do with your body from a purely physical point of view?

It will typically be something along the lines of you straightening your back, breathing calmly, smiling, relaxing, thinking everything will be fine and feeling positive about the future. Next time you're insecure, try copying this state by having the same body posture, thinking the same thoughts and doing the same things. It might feel silly at first if you haven't tried it before, but it works, because the body sends signals to your brain to improve your mood. By actively using your body posture and mimicking, you can fool your brain into thinking that you're happy. You can also find an energetic song that makes you happy, crank up the volume and dance all you can for five minutes. The latter I've done in periods when I was tired and needed to boost my energy before having to hold a coaching session with a client over the phone.

3. THE SPECIFIC APPROACH

The third exercise you can do to overcome fears and insecurities is to be more specific. Often, in our minds we can make a situation worse than it really is, and then we quickly lose perspective. By being specific, you direct your mind to see that it's not as bad as you've made it out to be.

1. Take a look at what you have to do, but fear will go wrong.
2. Write down:
   On a scale of 1 to 10, how likely is it to happen?
   How long is the problem likely to last, or how great will the damage be?
   What can you do to reduce the likelihood of it going wrong?

   For example, I was terribly nervous the first time I had to speak in front of many people. But when

I got specific about it, I found out that the likelihood of something going wrong wasn't that big, as I knew my subject matter well and was prepared. Worst-case scenario, I could read from my notes, and should that go wrong, the damage would be mostly to my ego and the participants, who would have been bored at worst – which they'd probably forget about quickly anyway. Life goes on. Last, but not least, I could reduce the likelihood of it going wrong by practicing and getting feedback from a performance coach I knew. It ended up going quite well. I was nervous and it could probably have gone better, but the audience was pleased and got what they came for.

Trial and Error

Your convictions are closely connected with what you do, and the way you perceive what happens to you. They can either give you support to succeed in your business, or they can be a huge obstacle. There is one conviction in particular that I believe is important to have if you want to succeed in being self-employed. It's a basic attitude that can help you in the face of adversity and what for many people is the difference between reaching for their goals or giving up. This attitude is that it's okay to make mistakes. Many self-employed people start to doubt themselves because they don't get results soon enough. Their natural conclusion is that what they're doing isn't working, so they should be doing something else.

It's great being solution-oriented. Most have heard of Einstein's wise words, "Insanity is doing the same thing over and over again expecting different results." As none of us want to be labelled insane, we try something new, of course. It's definitely important to measure your results, and tweak and improve what you're doing. Where many go wrong, however, is that they become impatient and change course before really knowing if what they're doing actually works.

It's a bit like if a person who has never run before takes advice from an 'iron-woman' on how to prepare for a marathon and gives up after a month of training because she is not able to run the distance yet. Instead of continuing her training, she thinks it's not working and tries another method instead.

This behaviour results in many self-employed people being stressed by jumping from one strategy to another, without succeeding in anything. They write a bit on Facebook, hardly get any likes and stop doing it. They send out newsletters without selling anything and reach the conclusion that it doesn't work. They send invitations to a free lecture but no one signs up, and then start worrying that there isn't a market for what they have to offer.

If you train your mind to realize that it's okay to make mistakes and to keep at it to do better the second time around, then you won't have to waste a lot of time worrying and looking for alternatives. Instead, you can focus on getting better.

The truth of the matter is that everyone who starts from scratch – who doesn't come from a business where they already have clients, or isn't famous on TV or other media – starts small and grows from there. It's completely normal, and there's no shame in that. It's important to understand that it takes time to build up a business so you don't start with unrealistic expectations and believe there's something wrong with you or with your idea.

The first time I hosted an event for business mums, only two people signed up, and I chose to cancel it. Of course, I was frustrated, because it'd gone down the drain, but instead of giving up, I did more research on what makes people attend events. I tried with several smaller events and themes, and 10 months later, there were 100 participants at one of my events. If I'd stopped after my first effort,

I'd never have felt the pleasure of speaking before so many self-employed women and contributing to inspiring them.

When you're in the midst of it, ten months can seem like a long time. In this kind of situation, it is important to keep the big picture in mind. You're creating a business and a great life for yourself. It takes time and sometimes many tries, but the results are worth it.

Feeling your way and learning from your mistakes is frequently the way to do it when starting a business, especially when it's within a field where you don't have much previous experience.

Anna Bogdanova is a personal trainer, a coach, a teacher and the author of the Danish bestsellers Skyhøj forbrænding (*Sky High Fat-Burning*) and Veldrejet (*Well Shaped*). Over 6,000 women have completed her courses, and she's the leading figure in a business called De Uimodståelige (*The Irresistible*) that employs 31 people. Her journey as self-employed entrepreneur started in 2008. Before that, she worked as a project manager in a communications agency, where she was overcome with stress, went on sick leave and finally was fired. She was good enough at her job, but it drained her. In that same period, Anna trained too much in the fitness center and got too little sleep, so something finally snapped. "It was a time when I tried doing everything in half the time, without doing anything I really had a passion for," Anna says.

Anna didn't feel like going back to a similar job. She spoke with Jacob, whom she had been dating for a year at that time, and who is now her husband. He'd never been employed and had a different perspective on work.

"What else have you spent a lot of time on?" he asked her. The answer was training. Anna had started reading quite a lot about what they do in the US, she had taken part in conversations on online forums and acquired new knowledge on the subject. She found it helpful getting support from abroad for her own training and with the internet, the world was within her reach. All her research was really a distraction from all the other tasks she'd had at work. Instead of feeling bad about the time she'd spent on it, she turned it into her business.

"I'd started hanging out at Welcome Fitness; then I began helping out, and among other things, I measured the clients' body fat percentages. After some time, I was offered a job there as a personal trainer – the type of job Jacob had. However, I still wasn't quite myself. I continued struggling with stress-related problems, and I ended up promising too much. It was hard selling one class at a time, but I didn't fully trust my skills as a trainer, to offer my clients ten classes at a time."

"I made the classic mistakes, but I needed to practise working with people first, and find out what motivates them and creates results. After the first class with a client, I gave them too strenuous, fix-it-all plans, and they didn't come back, because it was just too much. If we bumped into each other afterwards, we both felt like failures – me, because my plans didn't hold water, and them, because they were embarrassed for not sticking to the plan," Anna says.

Anna started wondering if training could be done differently, because she found out that more and more women didn't respond to classic strength-training methods of one hour at a time, heavy weights and fewer carbs. She started reading up on stress psychology and learned that nothing works if the body is overloaded. So, she switched to training with 40 minutes of restoration and breathing exercises, and only 20 minutes strength training – and then her clients started to feel a change.

"During the first six months, there was a lot of trial and error, where I tried lots of new things. A lot of what should've worked, didn't work. I also discovered that some people developed digestive problems after following popular diet plans. We began to work on that, which meant, among other things, more carbs and less fibre. I started seeing a pattern of what worked for most, and what it took to avoid going back to square one when the course was over. I chose to abandon the idea of making an optimal plan, which was what my customers asked for, and instead, looked at their habits and how their overall health was."

In 2010, Anna got pregnant for the first time, and she gave birth to Valentin in April the following year. Anna remembers she thought she'd soon be back at work.

"I was naive enough to think that I could have two weeks' maternity leave and then get back to work. I had a hard time accepting that I couldn't, and that made it even worse. I tried to force it, but ended up collapsing. With a baby, and a shifting Circadian rhythm, I couldn't make one-to-one classes work, and had to cancel too many. It was so frustrating. I started taking a deeper look at what other options there were from a business point of view. I stumbled upon spiritual methods where it was all about manifesting, but it didn't work for me. Then I came across Business Bootcamp with three successful businesswomen, where, among other things, I learned more about product mixes, online marketing and PR."

Anna learned to create and market group training programs so that she could earn more money in the same amount of time.

Anna's first group was 'The 1200 Group', which consisted of one collective training class per week and the rest online. "I was taken aback with all the work it takes to make an online course. I mistakenly thought I'd get more freedom by having online products, but it is not passive income. The idea of making a funnel, like they show in marketing courses, and the customers simply come to you, doesn't work. You always have to be doing something. You can stick to it 24 hours a day, because the participants need to be motivated between training sessions so they don't relapse to old habits or lose their courage. I wanted to start by introducing one new habit a week to my clients. Then it turned into every other week, or more seldom, because there were a number of fundamental things that had to be changed first. For example, when your clients need to go to bed earlier to avoid getting tired, hungry or lose their willpower and start to eat too much or do the wrong things. It's not because people don't get it; you have to look at what happened earlier that day that makes them feel like they have to stay awake instead of going to bed. I had to lower my requirements for my clients and lower the bar; otherwise it was too frustrating for both parties. Since I've started, I've become more in sync with people, and I've realized that there's something called life that gets in the way of good intentions.

"In the beginning, I made budget plans that were not robust enough. I over-delivered like crazy, because I couldn't meet my deadlines for my clients, and I gave them too much extra information and things they could also do that they didn't really appreciate anyway. It was extremely frustrating. I tripped myself up and was close to giving up. It was a tough couple of years, where Jacob had to put in more hours to save us financially. I kept telling him that very soon I'd be earning more, that the money would come. He began to doubt that this would happen, which I can perfectly understand, because three years had passed by then," Anna explained.

Then, in 2013, Anna secured a book contract. A publisher, Mette Holbæk, who also owned a Business Bootcamp, realized that Anna had got hold of something special, so she asked her to visit the publishing house. The book contract gave Anna enough time to go in-depth and analyse her concept while writing Skyhøj forbrænding (*Sky High Fat-Burning*). She learned about social media marketing, and she feels that she succeeded with that because she loves her clients and she has a passion for helping them with their problems. She's also good at reading between the lines and distinguishing what they ask for from what they really need.

The book was published in 2014 and became a success. It promises great results in under seven weeks, with four 15-minute training sessions a week. In November of the same year, Anna created the 'Balder uden buler' (Bumpless Buttocks) course, which contains a lot of advice there was no room for in the book. The online course became a huge success, with 370 people subscribing instantly. All her mistakes and experience from the preceding years finally made sense and were now converted into products her clients still rejoice over.

Tenacity and Action

Anna's story shows tenacity and constant action are the way to succeed, which can be both good and bad when you have your own business. It's challenging, because you want to see quick results and your patience will be put to the test time and time again. The good thing about this is that it takes the pressure off individual actions – if you're aware of it. It's definitely not the one blog post, phone call or lecture that'll make you sell more, but the sum of all your actions over time will create a well-oiled business. So, it's not essential to do everything perfectly; rather, everything should be in order. The key is to learn from your mistakes as you go along.

Often, we pay too much attention to an individual action, and expect a lecture, or a fair or a meeting in particular to be decisive for our business. It can make an action seem too complicated, and we feel pressured and insecure because we feel the need to perform and be perfect. If you reduce the emphasis of each individual action, and realize the value of doing your best, you remove much of the pressure that often stops or stresses self-employed entrepreneurs.

Just imagine that you're training for a big race. It's not a single day of training that makes a difference in how quickly and painlessly you complete the race, it's the sum total of your training. The fact that you've done it in a goal-oriented way over a long period of time and followed a plan. That's what makes the difference.

The same goes for your business. Investing energy in doing a little bit every day will get you closer to your goals. Perfect doesn't exist. You have to look at the bigger picture. Being self-employed is a lifestyle, and your business a long-term project. The key to success is taking the time every day to do the most important tasks that will help you reach your goal. The work tasks you concentrate your time and attention on will grow and turn into something. The rest grinds to a halt. If you want to call businesses, do it every day; if you want to blog, write every day; if you want to become a good lecturer, then practice every day.

External Adversity

Sometimes adversity can come from the outside. You shouldn't be in fear of negative things happening to you. However, if they should occur, it is easier to deal with knowing that others have been there before you and that it's not the end of your business, but rather an unpleasant phase you can and will get through.

In her 14 years as a business owner, Louise has seen her ups and downs. The first challenges occurred before she had even opened her first sushi restaurant.

"I had found the first location, made the payment and started to decorate the place when the pizza owner next door filed a complaint, saying it was illegal competition, opening a restaurant in the same building. At that time I didn't want to start my business with a lawsuit, so I decided to find a new place instead. Obviously, it was a blow and a huge setback, but it didn't keep me from following my dream."

This was just a small taste of adversity as a business owner. In 2013, Louise was contacted by a trade union that wanted to negotiate the work conditions for some of their members who were employed at Letz Sushi. After negotiating for a year without getting anywhere, the situation became a public affair.

The conflict hit the headlines in the newspapers in 2014 and people were demonstrating in front of the restaurants.

"It was very brutal and it felt like a personal attack on me. I couldn't have prepared for it. I didn't know it could be like that and I hadn't done anything wrong."

Louise was opposed to the agreement because it was too expensive. It would have resulted in the company having to close down within a couple of months and in the long run she would have had to dismiss 150 employees in total.

Other unions sympathized, which meant that certain supplies and even mail wasn't delivered to Letz Sushi.

Louise also had an external communications agency help her with PR. The intention was to get professional advice, but she also learned in the process to trust herself and her gut feeling more.

"The agency put me in situations that were out of my comfort zone. I accepted to do interviews I didn't feel like doing and I crossed my own boundaries. I let myself get carried away with their ideas and afterwards felt bad about doing it," Louise remembers.

The conflict went on for years and only stopped after Louise left the company last year.

"As it went on for a really long time, I had to distance myself from it, and mentally focus on separating work from my personal life. I had to see it as a job and remind myself that it wasn't my whole life."

At first Louise wanted to handle the situation by herself, but found out the importance of reaching out and asking for help. She got massive support from the chairman of her board and also from most of her employees.

"It was a big relief to be able to rely on somebody else, and as women we should be better at asking for help earlier in the process instead of trying to carry the whole weight ourselves," Louise stresses.

In the beginning it felt like the end of the world, but you learn to live with it, and, as time went by, Louise realized that if you take it one day at a time, life actually does go on. "Even though you can't control how long it will last, you can control how much you let adversity impact your everyday life."

"When things get rough, I tell myself that it's only work, and quickly make the decision to move on. Fortunately I've always been good at separating work and family and been able to enjoy my time off. Even though, as a passionate entrepreneur, your work and personal life will often be intertwined, you should never let work-related problems ruin quality time with your family," Louise explains.

So, pick your battles wisely in the face of external adversity and criticism. It can be very emotional and draining to fight, and it's not guaranteed that you'll win in the end. Sometimes you have to ignore them, even if you're right and they're wrong. At times of conflict, a key consideration should be if it's worth your time and energy, or if it's better to let it go and move on to what's important.

Louise Ferslev, a new mom and the woman behind MyMonii, a pocket money app for children, also experienced a wild first few years in business, with both bitter adversity and great success. The media has often praised her as a young woman in the tech sector, and if you read the articles, you'd be tempted to believe that the funding came easily to her and everything has been smooth sailing. The reality is very different.

Louise got the idea for MyMonii in 2013 while she was studying, and she worked on the project alongside her studies. The idea behind MyMonii was to develop a mobile app where parents could transfer pocket money to their children and set up tasks for rewards. The children can have an overview of earned, saved and spent money, and get an idea of how money functions in the real world. To begin with, the app was an account between parents and the children without real money, with a view to one day connecting to a 'prepaid' debit card that works for real.

"To begin with, I held a lot of meetings to expand my network and establish new contacts that could help me proceed. I naively tried to ask for £200,000 – £300,000 right off the bat, and I wasn't particularly flexible in my negotiations. But I quickly learned that you can't raise that kind of money with a couple of PowerPoint slides."

Through a teacher from her college, she was introduced to Thor Angelo, an angel investor and a former entrepreneur, who was immediately interested in the idea. They met a couple times with another investor, who also was interested in the idea. At the time, Louise was a humble student, so when the more experienced businessmen suggested they only contribute £6,000 each, she felt out of her league, because that was a huge amount for her. The investors hadn't really expected her to contribute financially; all they expected from her was her work. "Even so, I still insisted on investing £3,000, so my involvement in the company was recorded on paper. It was money I didn't have, so I got credit from the bank. It was an expensive loan, and I was working on the side to pay it back quickly."

Louise had several partners along the way. Two partners abandoned ship before the app went from project to business. One left quietly, because he wanted to spend more time with his family. The other partner's exit was a tad more dramatic.

Louise recounts: "We didn't think he worked or contributed enough to the business, as he also had a job on the side, so we wanted him out. He didn't agree to that, and it cost us dearly to get rid of him. It was like a covert operation, like something out of a movie. He'd gained access to my emails and read them, so he knew what our next strategic move was. When I found out what was going on, I was mad as hell and reported it to the police. But, although I was angry, I didn't wish that for him; after all, he is a father. Instead, I encouraged him to not take the case further; he agreed and took back the £5,000 he'd invested."

"It was crazy. I was young, 24-year-old student, and they were 40-year-old men with power struggles that were totally different to what I was used to or had experienced. It was a clash between the inexperienced and the experienced. If Thor Angelo hadn't been willing to personally pay the legal fees, we would've had to close the business. It was a giant circus that drew focus away from what we were doing and delayed the project. This taught me that it's important to have contracts in place for everything!

"We started by developing a skeletal version of the app and tested it with ten families," Louise continues. "However, it never quite took off, so we found ten more, got in-depth feedback, learned a lot, and continued to develop and test the app in a closed environment. Thor Angelo had a good network, and he fixed meetings with Seed Capital, one of Denmark's biggest investment funds. At the time, MyMonii had just over 100 families actively using the app. There were enough users to convince investors to fund the project and in the end we got £50,000 in total, and Thor invested £10,000 in the business."

Following these investments, in 2015, MyMonii started as a limited company. Although it sounds like a lot of money, it was just enough to cover the expenses incurred in 2016 – then Louise had to raise more money. She began two months before the money was due to run out and quickly realized that there was not enough time to achieve the sum required.

"It takes many meetings to establish good relationships and trust. We were tremendously pressed for time, and every-one I spoke to was not interested in investing. At the same time, I was then heavily pregnant, and I knew it would be even harder to raise money in my state. How would I be able to convince anyone to invest in my firm when I'd soon be leaving and didn't know how life with a baby would be?

"I ended up running out of money. I had no option but to be honest with my employees and explain that I wouldn't be able to pay their salaries the following month. Unfortunately, and understandably, they chose to leave. So, there I was, alone and heavily pregnant. It sucked, I thought, I have to close the business. It felt awful, and I felt terrible about it. Normally I'm quite proactive, but adversity made me passive." But, luckily, all the work and all the meetings Louise had held earlier had left their mark.

"I'd been a fair bit in the media with articles, and due to this I was contacted by an accountant who'd seen I was looking for investors. We met for a coffee and it turned out that he had at least two clients willing to invest in my app. The first one he introduced me to definitely wasn't impressed, and the person didn't want to invest in my business.

"In the meantime, people from my own network, who'd followed me on social media, approached me. There were two guys who wanted to invest £25,000 each. I immediately accepted both offers. After that, I had a meeting with the other person the accountant knew. It was okay, because I was no longer desperate since I had money again, and we had a calm and serene chat about life in general, and hardly spoke about the company. To my great surprise, he came back the day after and offered to invest £150,000! It was almost too good to be true. His evaluation of the business was even higher, so by the end of June, we had £200,000 in our account. It was insane, the way we went from one extreme to the other. When things go well, it's awesome. The good definitely overshadows the bad. Luckily, the big challenges are fewer and apart from that, there are only the small problems that you can solve on a day-to-day basis," Louise explains.

Accept the Uncomfortable

When I had just started my second business with a girlfriend, I met with a couple friends from my coaching course to run through some ideas. They'd both been self-employed for a couple years, and they immediately challenged me on how I'd get my first clients. At first, I used classic arguments, like I'd first have to get a company registration number, find premises, create a homepage and so on. Good, valid reasons not to concern myself with clients just yet. In my view, at least. But every time we met, they kept insisting on sales and clients, and I ended up running out of things I had to do first.

After some time, it reached a point where I didn't want to meet with them unless I had a client, or at least a few meetings in my calendar – it made me more nervous than getting started did. My homepage wasn't ready, and I was far from securing premises, but I made up my mind that I was going to show them. The next time we'd meet, I would be able to show results on the client front. I made a one-page PDF that briefly presented me and my business, and decided I'd go to my clients instead of waiting for them to come to me. Subsequently, I identified and contacted 20 institutions, which were all near to my home, offering to coach their managers.

I didn't have the courage to cold call, because I didn't have any references for this kind of work, and I came from an unknown firm that was brand new.

So, I locked myself up in my bedroom with my phone, the list of institutions I wanted to contact, and a piece of paper where I'd written what to say. I was determined not to come out of my bedroom before I had fixed a meeting or at least gone through the entire list. I was uncomfortable and unsure, but my tiny ten-line script got me through the calls and I ended up fixing four meetings, of which three became clients. One client even agreed to a contract that was financially big enough to cover several months' pay for me. Finally, at that stage I knew I could stand tall when I met my friends again.

I was lucky enough to have friends who pushed me to act quickly. Many of those I meet who've just started a business run out of motivation or money before they're seriously ready to plunge into the fight for clients, and sometimes it's too late.

When something is new and you're not sure of the outcome, it'll feel uncomfortable, like a pair of beautiful, new shoes that have to be broken in. Naturally, you have to do it all the same, either by taking baby steps so it's not too overwhelming, or by blocking the exits, like I did, when I went into my room. You get better at it, and it feels better the more you do it. Today, I have so many good experiences under my belt that I find it fun calling businesses and I even teach self-employed people how to do it best.

Louise from MyMonii definitively recognizes the value of self-development and explains: "My comfort zone has moved by a huge amount since I started. Back then, holding meetings was a big deal and I felt totally star-struck when sitting opposite businessmen with lots of money, as I would get extremely nervous. Today, it's not a problem.

I've also learned how to speak at events and in front of big groups, so this is almost a pleasant experience for me in comparison.

"I still get nervous sometimes, and to calm my nerves I always start by chatting with the participants so we get the conversation going and I don't have to present myself like a total stranger.

"Now successful businesspeople have a great effect on me, it makes me feel special and confident to know that they are present and they believe in and are interested in MyMonii."

Courage Can Be Trained

Being brave is about listening to yourself, instead of your fears or what others may say about you. Everyone can become courageous; you just need to work at it and the more you do, the better.

Mother of two and self-employed entrepreneur, Pia Nissen Tylak has consciously and successfully trained her courage. Pia, who has been self-employed for over 20 years and has run three well-functioning businesses, explains, "I wanted to train my courage, which was a quality I felt I lacked. It's sad that most people forget their strengths and gifts when they're in the grip of fear. A good exercise that I use is taken from Jung's work with psychology. It's about how we see our own qualities in others. You can unwrap your own strengths by looking at the qualities of the people you idolize, the people you look up to, the people who fascinate you.

"For example, one of my idols is Richard Branson, who started with nothing, to go on and become the successful entrepreneur and philanthropist he is today. Looking at his qualities, part of what characterizes him is that he's true to his heart and possess great courage," Pia says.

Pia therefore decided that she wanted to meet Richard Branson. So, she wrote to his organization many times but never got a response. Then she learned that the Danish stock exchange had invited him to Denmark to give a speech on reducing global warming, but the event was only for members of stock exchange Executive Club, and the membership alone cost £800. But Pia was firmly determined to establish contact.

"Somehow, I managed to find the £800 and signed up to attend the event. I wrote a letter to him, and I asked the organizers if I could give it to him, but they declined."

When Richard Branson was done with his presentation, he asked if anyone in the room had any questions. There were a thousand men in suits and only a few women, so Pia thought she might be noticed if she stuck her hand up in the air. She really had nothing to lose, and her goal was to talk to him.

"I raised my hand, and was handed a microphone, but instead of asking a question about global warming, I told him how he was my role model, and that I wanted to give him my letter, to thank him for being such an inspiration."

The director of the stock exchange, Leif Beck Fallesen, looked displeased, but Branson took it in his stride and invited Pia to the stage to deliver her letter. She went to shake his hand to greet him, but he took her in his arms and gave her a smacking kiss on the mouth, and in a sassy manner asked if there were other women who had something to say to him. The letter created an opening with Branson's secretary, who later arranged for Pia to interview him for her book.

"If you don't have courage, and you don't take the bull by the horns, you can end up missing so much in life. What do we have to lose? Often, you only lose what you don't need in your life anyway, and get more on track instead," Pia says.

Another person Pia was keen to meet was another one of her role models, the American entrepreneur, business coach, and writer, Tony Robbins. She attended one of his events in London, which had over 6,000 attendees. As she had done with Branson, Pia had written numerous letters to his organization – and received rejections from all of them. She was determined not to leave until she spoke to him. She knew she'd succeed, because her wish came from her heart.

At the event, she came across a booth allowing VIP club members to take pictures with Tony Robbins. The membership fee, however, cost a whopping £35,000, so she gave up on that idea. During lunch, she heard an announcement that Robbins was going to answer three questions later, if people stayed behind after the talk. That's what Pia and 4,000 others did. Pia was not chosen to ask the first or the second question, and she had to think quick on her feet to find a way of being allowed to ask the third question. She'd tried to position herself near the stage, but that hadn't helped. She saw a table nearby and climbed on top of it and began waving her arms. A bold move that ended up working!

"The Danes who were with me thought I was crazy and embarrassing, but it worked, and the microphone was passed on to me. And I asked: 'You say not to give up, and to follow your dream. My dream is to get a picture and an interview with you for my book. How can I get it even though you say you won't give interviews?'"

Tony Robbins agreed to a photo on the roof, and his security people followed her there, where he stood together with his wife.

"People often only express their prejudice when they see me follow my dream. I'm not afraid of losing face, as long as I can look myself in the mirror and feel proud and know that I've been brave," Pia says.

Pia's examples show the value and importance of courage. Courage requires you to push your boundaries, and that's something a self-employed entrepreneur has to work with to develop a business and reach their goals.

Exercise: Become More Courageous

Take baby steps: the easiest way of working on your courage is to take one small step at a time, so that it doesn't feel frightening or overwhelming. If, for example, you want to get better at public speaking, you can start by practicing in front of the mirror, then do it in front of two people, five people, ten people, and so on. That way your confidence grows with the task and gets used to it.

Frequent action: Do something, not necessarily work related, outside of your comfort zone on a daily or a weekly basis. By regularly challenging yourself, you'll discover that you're perfectly capable of doing more that you think. Every time you succeed, you get a little adrenaline kick, and your courage grows, slowly but surely. It might even prompt you to do more. If you find it hard getting started on your own, find a friend who'll play along, and challenge each other.

The Difference Between Fear and Lacking Skills

Self-employment is a process of self-development that involves a steep learning curve. You will constantly be faced with your own fear and insecurity and you will be pushed out of your comfort zone.

When faced with a task or an action you're not in the mood for, it's important to identify the reason. Is it fear or a weakness? From my clients and through my own experience, I know that fear and weaknesses can hinder development, and so they must be handled. First and foremost, it is important to have the ability to differentiate between them.

A weakness is when you're not particularly good at something, but which doesn't give you a strong emotional reaction. It can be tasks you're okay with doing but take you a long time, or the result won't be excellent, since you're not particularly good at it.

Fear manifests itself when a task or a decision give you a strong emotional reaction; you create distractions, feel unwell or find excuses not to do it. Maybe you seek refuge in your favourite bad habit to numb your feelings, like shopping, food, alcohol, cigarettes, sugar, TV or Facebook.

Fear is tricky, because your brain is good at deceiving you with distractions and excuses that seem real enough, but if you're honest with yourself, you can definitely tell the difference between fear and weaknesses.

In my case, a weakness could be that I'm not particularly detail-oriented. In my first business, I did all my invoicing on a spreadsheet, and wasted oodles of time printing them, finding new mistakes, correcting them and printing them again before I could put them in an envelope and send them. Luckily, I have an online system today that does the job for me, but I still get help with the bookkeeping, as I overlook too many important details. I might be able to learn to do it on my own, but it really is a waste of my time, and my time is better spent doing what I have a passion for.

Fear for me could be public speaking. To start with, I wasn't very good at it, but contrary to checking details and invoicing, it's something I want to do. I'm an extrovert, I love being with other people, and I want to share my experience. Instead of shying away from holding lectures, I went all in – one step at a time. First with smaller groups, then learning from a performance coach and a voice trainer.

I was insanely nervous the first time I spoke in front of 100 people, and I can't remember much about it, but I know it went well. Nowadays I relish such speaking opportunities, even though I still have butterflies in my stomach.

The important thing here is that you distinguish between your fears and weaknesses. If you don't, and you don't learn how to handle them, you risk losing valuable time and missing out on fantastic experiences.

Pernille Birkenfeldt also came out of her comfort zone with the help of a mentor. She'd been an accountant for nine years when she decided to become self-employed, and she set up a business that would help other self-employed entrepreneurs with their finances.

"It had to feel solid, because I'm used to settling in my office and hiding behind the brand. Just being me was a big step out of my comfort zone," Pernille remembers.

"You have to give out so much of yourself as a self-employed consultant. It has really surprised me how many times, and in how many ways, you have to say things before anything happens. In this respect, I've moved my boundaries and become better at keeping to the goals I set for myself, for example, when I write newsletters or make Facebook posts." Pernille says.

"All along, I've worked with a mentor who can challenge me and with whom I discuss my issues and ideas. We can talk about why something is difficult or easy and what lies behind that feeling. It's nice to have someone with whom you can make agreements that you try to adhere to, so I can act towards the goals I set myself instead of letting fear stop me."

Exercise: Differentiating Between Strengths, Weaknesses and Fears

Start by making a list of your work tasks.

- What do you have to do? Sales, marketing, product development, customer service, accounting, communication ... ?
- What skills do you need to be able to solve these tasks? Accounting, for example, requires a flair for details and knowledge of bookkeeping, marketing would require you to be good at writing, sales may require you to be good at reaching out.

Look through the list and divide your tasks. On one side, make a list of what you like to do or what you're good at. On the other side list which tasks drain you or those you're not particularly good at.

Look at the tasks you don't like, these are your weaknesses. For each of these, decide if you should outsource, or get help to overcome your fear, or have professional training so that you feel more secure in what you're doing overall.

Keep this overview. In Step 3, we will be looking at how you can optimize your resources and continue working with task allotment.

STEP 2

Develop Your Strategy

A Strategy That Makes Sense

Your vision comprises the dreams or desires you have for the future. Your strategy is the plan you implement to ensure your vision becomes a reality. Your strategy will help you take active steps in a concrete and measurable fashion to achieve your dreams.

Set Specific Goals for Your Business

It's hard to try to predict the future, so when setting your goals, it's important to be realistic in terms of the status of your business and the means you have at your disposal. If you're like most self-employed people, myself included, you're probably impatient and want everything to happen quickly and are quite optimistic that things will turn out all right. That combination of impatience and optimism can make it difficult to set realistic goals, and a good way to put things into perspective is to run your ideas by another person.

One of my clients needed help to earn £36,000 for the following year. She'd earned £34,000 the previous year. But she didn't see a great advancement from where she was to where she wanted to be. To tackle this, we talked about how she could raise the bar without too much effort, since she had a good existing client base to build upon.

At the same time, another client of mine wanted to earn £100,000 in the course of the following year. She had just received her company registration number, but had not yet developed a list of clients. With the services she wanted to offer, it could be done, but it would require a lot of hard work, and she'd have to invest a sizeable amount of money in marketing to be able to do it that quickly. By putting things into perspective and being realistic, she realized that she didn't really need that much money. She reached the conclusion that she'd rather move her goal further into the future and also spend more time with her daughter.

Whether your goal is £20,000 or £200,000 is beside the point; the result depends on what you're selling, your client base and what means you have at your disposal.

Having ambitious goals is great, but if you don't want to work 90 hours a week, perhaps they should be more realistic and set out over a longer term. Being realistic means you will also have time for your family and that you don't end up running yourself into the ground. In the big picture, slowing down the pace at which you reach your goals won't make a huge difference. The most important thing is that you've felt good about the process you take to reach them. In reality, most people often find that it takes longer to reach their goals because of unexpected things cropping up that they had not foreseen when they started.

How much do you want to earn? In three months, six months, a year, two years? When you've set your turnover or earnings goals, it's important to break them down and specifically look at how many clients or sold products they correspond to.

For example, let's say you want to earn £50,000 in one year, excluding VAT. Depending on what you're selling, for example, one-to-one sessions at £50 per hour, or a course at £3,333 per seat or eBooks at £25 each, there will be a big difference in how you achieve this goal.

In this case, reaching a £50,000 goal would require you to sell 1,000 one-to-one sessions, 15 seats on the course, or 2,000 eBooks. Again, by being realistic, we can say that you will be actively selling for ten months of the year –

so that low seasons, holidays and illness are taken into account. This would mean that each month you would have to sell and hold 100 classes, 1.5 course seats or 200 eBooks. Whether or not these are realistic goals and how much work it will require from you depends on where you are today with your business, but it's clear to see that selling 15 seats a year for a course will be much easier and manageable than selling and holding 100 one-to-one sessions a month. Furthermore, you must add up your expenses (salaries, rent, production costs), and then the profit and the money you will earn for yourself.

If you don't know the math by heart, do it now. You may not be a wiz at bookkeeping, taxes and all the rest, but you have to know how much you have to sell to be able to reach your goals. When you do the math, you'll quickly be able to see if your prices are too low, if you can make ends meet, or if you have to make a different product mix. Maybe the price for your clients is still £50 per hour, but you have groups of five instead of one-to-one sessions, so you earn more, or you find another supplier for your products so that you can buy them cheaper and earn more by charging the client the same.

Now it's your turn:
- How much do you want to earn a month?
- How many/which products or services do you have to sell to reach this goal?
- Does it seem realistic?

Bad Advice and Misleading Myths

Nowadays we have access to a lot of resources online where people always want to offer advice. This can make it difficult to identify and follow the best route.

In many ways, I was lucky when I started my first business in Paris back in 2006. The crisis hadn't yet happened, and I was tremendously optimistic about the possibilities. I was far away from family and friends, and thus my decisions were not influenced by their thoughts. I wasn't on Facebook at that time, so I didn't really compare myself to anyone, or try to copy anyone's idea, either. This meant that my business partner and I started our recruiting firm based on the possibilities we saw and the services we wanted to offer.

My partner and I had no background in HR, but we could tell there was a need in the market and found solutions as we went along. Of course, we made mistakes – and learned from them – but none was so big that it had long-term consequences. However, we had fun, the business grew, and two years later, when I wanted to move to Denmark, I could sell my share of the firm.

Some thought it was a bit of a gamble starting a firm in Paris at the age of 25, but luckily, I was unaffected by my surroundings and driven by my own passion, which is a great starting point when setting up a business, as it requires a great amount of drive. Most of those who want to advise you on your business are really well-intentioned but don't know the first thing about what they're saying. They speak due to their own fears or something they've heard about, but not based on concrete experiences in starting up a company.

One of the reasons my recruiting firm in Paris was so successful was the fact that I learned from people who had hands-on experience and were in the midst of creating their own successful businesses and were a couple of years ahead of me in terms of experience.

There are lots of people who want to offer you advice, but only listen to those who have relevant experience within the field they're talking about. That way, you'll save yourself a lot of time and you'll be spared many pointless considerations and frustrations.

The Digital Marketing Trap

The internet has become an invaluable resource for business of all sizes and kinds, but it has also become an impenetrable jungle of advice on how to do just about anything, particularly online marketing. There are loads of experts who tell you that writing newsletters, blogs, Facebook posts, or setting up webinars and increasing your SEO are the key to many clients and a passive income. They create the impression that you hardly have to work to earn money – the money simply rolls into your account while you're sleeping, on holiday or at a café with your friends.

On the one hand, much of the advice seems sound enough. It makes good sense that you can reach more people online because everybody can make a more or less good homepage for free, and social media platforms are commonly used and help to establish a dialogue with your potential clients.

There's nothing wrong with expert advice on digital marketing, even if you're an established business with a good client base. Digital marketing provides a fantastic way to reach clients and sell services cheaper and with less effort, since a great portion of the workflow can be automated. So, it's quite true, there are many possibilities nowadays.

However, as self-employed individual with a small client base, the reality is a tad different in relation to digital marketing. There's no shortage of possibilities, but they're not all equally relevant when you're starting your business, and it can be hard finding out what's best to start with.

The challenge, however, and the thing that only a few people realize before they started is that digital marketing is a daily task. Just like you have to run several times a week to become good at running, see results, and become better, you have to write newsletters, notices, create webinars, or whatever you've chosen to do just as assiduously to see results. If you stop, nothing will happen. That requires a lot of your creativity and your productivity, because it does matter what you post online.

Today, immeasurable amounts of information are produced and shared online, and we're truly part of a modern digital culture where, in a matter of seconds, we decide to click away if something doesn't grab our attention. Therefore, it's not enough to share your pearls of wisdom – it also has to be done the right way.

This is the part where some people snap. Even if we want to share our wisdom, and to begin with we're inspired and highly motivated to achieve results, it quickly becomes a heavy chore day after day – if it's Facebook, sometimes a number of times a day (preferably four, if you ask the experts) – or week after week, to have to come up with new content. Content that maybe gets a couple of likes or comments, but rarely translates into real sales. All of a sudden, you feel trapped in a new online hamster wheel that you didn't even know existed, and you begin to wonder if there's any point in continuing. This is when you start taking one course after the other, in the hopes of becoming a wiz at Facebook, a genius at SEO, a newsletter ninja or whatever the creative brains have called their latest, most revolutionary course.

You spend all of your time attracting the right clients online, while quietly asking yourself if it was the reason you became self-employed, when the dream was doing something you have a passion for – not sitting in front of a screen, writing posts that sound increasingly devoid of substance. As an added frustration, on top of everything, the online universe is a visual snapshot of other people's lives that tempt you to believe that other people are on top of everything and successful. You're are left feeling that 'if the others can, then I'll also succeed in just a little while', and that you are the only nitwit that hasn't broken the code – but you don't dare say that out loud, because then others will see what a failure you are. It's a shame. What I've learned is that most of us struggle and that it isn't easy for anyone. We just don't have the guts to talk about it.

There's nothing wrong with any of us; we just lack relevant and decisive knowledge on how the internet and sales psychology really works. I see this with my clients and in my own business; the internet works when it's part of a larger, coherent strategy that is very goal-oriented and long term. It takes time to get results and build up a business, and there must be focus and a common thread in your strategy.

Define Your Target Group

A key element to succeeding with your communication, whether it's online or not, is knowing your clients. They are the ones who are going to buy your services, and who, ultimately, make it possible for you to live off your business. Many entrepreneurs are afraid of losing potential clients, and so wrongly believe that they have to approach everyone. However, reality is different. We live in a world where we're bombarded with information from all sides: radio, TV, magazines, newspapers, social media, the internet, etc., where knowledge is easily accessible, and we can effortlessly zap away. It requires you to plan and execute a clear and direct message to the right potential clients if you want to grab their attention for more than five seconds. Furthermore, it takes time and requires a lot of communication before anyone buys anything from you. There are a number of key factors that must be in place for anyone to make any kind of purchase:

1. A fundamental trust: First of all, we must trust the product or the person. The more expensive your product or service, the more it will need time and/or personal involvement for the potential client to trust.

You need to spend time building a relationship first and show that you, or your product, can create value for your customer.

2. An imminent need: Second we have to have a need. Many decisions can be postponed, so even if people are interested, it doesn't mean they'll buy something from you right away. For that reason, a long time can pass before you get clients.

3. A good investment: Third, we have to get hold of the money. Usually, we find a way of getting money to buy the things that are really important. But it's up to you to explain to your clients, in a clear way, why they're making a good investment that they won't regret.

Since the majority of online communication is free of charge, and requires mostly your time, you can easily forget how important it is to be specific and sharp regarding your target group. When you have to talk about all this and establish a relationship with potential clients, you have to know who they are, what is important for them, and where they are, so that you can find the right arguments and communicate in the right places. Otherwise, you can easily waste a lot of time, and a lot of money, without getting new clients.

As an aid to defining your target group, you can try this: Imagine you're offering massages. In principle, everyone can profit from massages, but there's a big difference as to where and how you will communicate and sell them, depending on if they are for injured sportsmen, pregnant women or pensioners. The choice of words and pictures will be very different, depending on which target group you're addressing. When defining your target group, you must look at their problems, challenges, desires and dreams.

You must understand their values and convictions so you can tell them what value you're offering them. It can be difficult working in-depth with your target group, and most business owners spend a long time on that before getting it right, but you will find out that your work becomes much easier when you know whom you're addressing. In most cases, your clients, or your target group, resemble you, and this makes it easier identifying their needs, values, desires, problems and convictions.

If your clients don't resemble you, it's even more important that you talk to them, so they tell you in their own words what is important for them.

> Describe who your clients are in relation to what you're offering.
> - What problems or challenges do they have?
> - What are the symptoms of their problems?
> - What results do they want?
> - What needs do they have?
> - What are their dreams?

We wish to maintain a certain self-image, and most of our actions reflect that. Your clients' values should tell you something about who they are as people, their identity, and what the most important things are for them. You know how it is: some women only buy organic and environmentally friendly products, while for others it's important that it's expensive, gorgeous and a specific brand, or else that it's functional and cheap. It's all about who we want to be. That's why the founder of Ikea, for example, Ingvar Kamprad, bought his clothes at car boot sales and drove around in an old Volvo even though he could afford to buy a luxury car. It was clearly important for him to be true to his identity, despite the fact that he became one of the world's richest men.

Therefore, it's important you ask yourself these questions:
- What is most important for my clients?
- What convictions do they have?
- What values do they emphasize?

Last, but not least, consider how your clients communicate and talk to them in their language, and choose pictures, layouts or decorations that appeal to them. You might be direct and emphasize facts, but your clients might prefer a less blunt approach.

Find out which of these four client types most resembles your clients, and adapt your communication accordingly:

1. The dominating, decisive types, who are very direct in their communication. Their focus is on results, and they make their decisions based on facts.
2. The imaginative, extrovert types, who are particularly interested in new things, possibilities and people, who are very informal in their communication and spontaneous in their decisions.
3. The social types, who focus on relationships and processes. They're interested in how other people feel, and they base their decisions on feelings.
4. The more introverted types, who emphasise thoroughness and data, and make rational decisions based on facts.

When you know who your target group is, you'll feel that it's significantly easier and less time-consuming finding out where and how to communicate with them.

Pernille Birkenfeldt experimented by choosing a target group she didn't have much experience with.

"Economics was really my mainstay. I visited businesses and got clients through my network from when I was an accountant. That gave me economic stability and room to experiment. I tried to speak about something I didn't know enough about, namely introverted people, because I'd been inspired to do so after having taken part in an online course. On Facebook, everybody sells online courses with a couple of steps and hey presto, you're living the life. Real life is not like that. All kinds of nonsense crops up and brings the process to a screeching halt.

"It's harder to be successful when we're trying to earn money on something other than what you're good at. I was a newly trained coach, and I wasn't brave enough to market myself as an expert. I took to social media to see what others in this space were doing. I couldn't press through. I had a mentor who helped me, so the exterior looked perfect with a great homepage. Introverts recognized the issues I was referring to, but it never turned into business. I spent a year and a half on that, and was close to chucking it all in and applying for a job.

"On one occasion, my mentor asked me if I was certain that this was what I wanted to do with my life. We talked a number of times, and it was hard for me to find out what the right thing was for me, so I put it aside. At the time, I was a member of an online network, where some people asked questions about finances and money. I answered them because it was something I knew a lot about and it was easy for me to answer. My mentor pointed that I should continue in that direction, so I asked the women following the 'thread' in the discussion whether they'd like a session on finances and three of them said yes at once. Finally, I got the 'flow' feeling that I'd heard others talk about, where it feels easy and clients come willingly because I'm passionate and credible at what I do. It's important to dare to trust your intuition and adjust. If something feels burdensome, it is burdensome! It's a sign that something isn't right and needs fixing. It might be hard work, but it has to be the fun kind of hard work. Now I help entrepreneurs with their finances, and it's a breeze compared to the introverts. I do it my way, not like a boring accountant, but as myself, over a cup of tea," Pernille says.

Besides knowing your target group, you must also choose one that you like so you feel it's fun in the long run. I once spoke to a woman who said she was sure that she could earn a lot of money if she helped rich, pampered, upper-class women with their problems.

The question is, however, whether these types of women would want help from her when she speaks of them in such a derogatory way. As I listened to her, I got the distinct impression that she didn't like them; she just wanted to get her hands on their money. Of course, it's important you like who you're selling to and that you have good chemistry with them.

Customer-Focused Growth

When you're faced with having to develop a new product or a new service, communication with your clients is key. One of the women who created results by talking to her clients is Anna Bogdanova.

"I believe in the value of customer surveys. You must always ask your clients what their challenges are and what they need help with. Start when your idea is in its infancy and don't take anything for granted. Everything changes every year, the market changes, and things always turn out differently than our expectations. My clients don't necessarily answer the same way two years in a row, because their needs and challenges are constantly evolving, other products have come on the market, new trends have appeared, and they've acquired more experience and so on. I've had to shelve many ideas and products that I thought were good, because my clients' feedback was not what I'd expected. I never look at what the competition does or doesn't do. I don't just do what I like, either. I wouldn't have gotten this far without asking my clients. I created a free Facebook group to follow up on those who did the Bumpless Buttocks exercise programme, and for those who bought *Sky High Fat-Burning* because I wanted to see how they used the book.

"Nowadays, I have much more experience and can quickly decode the market. It's also helps being in dialogue with my clients in different online groups on a daily basis. Now it's easy for me to realize business visions, but it's been a long period of trial and error that's given me a good gut feeling. I do a lot of zigzagging in my decisions, which helps me to continuously adapt, based on the dialogue I have with my clients. Every day, I take in a lot of fresh data and interpret the trends based on my gut feelings," Anna says.

Based on all the information Anna gets from her clients, she's been able to create even more popular products and develop her business at great speed.

"*Sky High Fat-Burning* is the most minimalistic and easiest programme you can follow to get results from your training. Some people need more training and help, and may need to go for more than seven weeks, or those who are stressed, suffer from pain, infirmity and chronic disease. I thought of creating a one-year course for them, because I realized where the shoe pinches and what it takes to stick to the good habits, with fewer ups and downs."

"At the same time, clients who wished to further boost their weight loss asked if I could create a New Year's weight loss diet program. As a response, and as an alternative to ineffective low-calorie diets that exhaust them and have the opposite effect, I developed a new product, *21 dage til en sprødere silhuet (21 Days to a Thinner Silhouette)*, which is an accelerator programme. I also wrote the book *Veldrejet (Shapely)*, which contains more information than *Sky High Fat-Burning* and includes a lot from my Bumpless Buttocks course."

In connection with each product, Anna involved her clients and developed each accordingly from the start.

"Present your idea and always involve your clients in the process. That way they will feel seen and heard, and will get to know you better. You can then tailor relevant products to them. This approach requires confidence, professionalism and knowing what you're good at. It's an ongoing process, finding the frequency with the least resistance. I'm not saying there's no resistance, but you mustn't be afraid of easy solutions. It's all about finding a business model that suits your strengths. I don't think I would have been as successful had I only relied on what I had learned on the online courses I took. In my case, I found these to be rather passive, and my strength is speaking with my clients and providing them with support." Anna explained.

In 2016, Anna was ready to start selling her one-year course 'Uimodståelig' ('Irresistible'), and her business exploded. The clients who took part in the course needed more support, and Anna had to hire freelance coaches connected to her work on a permanent basis. "The participants faced more adversity than we'd imagined. We had to deal with pain, stress and fatigue. We had to provide them with all-round help to progress and develop good habits. But it's fantastic and so rewarding, assisting a client develop and stick to a new, better lifestyle."

"I know what I can help people with, but it's also a long and demanding process getting them to do it wholeheartedly, let go of their doubts, and believe that they have what it takes to get through the course. It's hard work, and we've also grown more grey hairs in the course of the last year. My small shop has now grown into 'The Irresistible' enterprise. Today I run it with my business partner, coach and dear friend, Louise Berner, and we have 31 employees. Together, we've helped approximately 6,000 women. I can look back on our journey and say that our competent, strong, interdisciplinary team lifted online training levels above the norm. Actually, I'm proud to say we've rebranded online training as a serious training and lifestyle process that creates lasting behavioural changes.

"I feel we've succeeded in having the individual at the core of our online universe – and that we have gone beyond the screen and into the lounges. Although technology can be frustrating at times, the 'human' experience we have created in our digital communities, as well as the relationships between our coaches and clients, are so warm, so precious and so strong that we can only praise technology for helping us get closer to one another and help so many people develop a stronger life," Anna says.

An important element in development is that you can't do everything alone, and no one becomes a success on their own. Anna doesn't doubt that for a moment.

"I'm very grateful for the confidence that our clients and followers have in us to enter their lives and help them. I wouldn't be able to do any of this without the help and support of my excellent team, who stand shoulder to shoulder, ready to do the work and catch the balls we throw in the air. It means so much that they believe in the dream and in the vision, for better and for worse. I have to admit, it's been a breath-taking year. And it hasn't been all fun and games. To be honest, at times it's been really hard work, but together we've made it so far!"

Anna also recognizes the value of having a skilled partner. "Louise is our beacon of light. She has a passion for allowing each employee to explore their unique strengths and contribute where they're the very best. She's the reason why the team is thriving, developing, and has the capacity to include, guide and be there for our clients. Louise makes sure the whole team is on board with the course we stake out, without getting too swept away by the changes we make to the course to meet clients' needs.

"This may sound odd, but I also give myself a pat on the shoulder. It feels awesome seeing my long-standing dream of helping women who, until now, found it hard to follow traditional fitness programmes get a better life and a stronger body through sheer determination. That dream is now reality."

Four Phases to Get Customers

When you've identified your key customers, it becomes easier to prepare a plan to target them and get more of them. There are many models for strategizing, so it can quickly become too exhausting and unfathomable. It may even feel like something you just have to do to keep the bank happy, but it's not something you can really use in your everyday dealings.

That is why I recommend you to set up your strategy based on the 'Know, Like, Trust, Buy' principle. In simple terms, the premise for people to buy something from someone is to know them first, and to like them and trust them before they buy. If you try to sell to someone when trust hasn't yet been established, it will feel uncomfortable for them and for you. This is easier to keep to and makes it less likely that you will forget an important stage. No matter how many clients you have at the moment, you'll be able to use this method to get more.

You can set up a strategy according to the four phases – 'Know, Like, Trust, Buy' – which determines how developed and experienced your business is and where you should act.

Phase One: Know

This phase has to do with visibility. It's about your visibility and target group discovering you, your business or your products. Here you have to focus on catching their attention where they are. It can be through advertising, PR and trade fairs or, if you're selling to a company, by contacting them directly.

Many self-employed entrepreneurs are tempted to start by focusing this communication on themselves and their method or product. But, it's really far too early in the process for that. Your future clients aren't sitting around waiting to hear about you. They have a problem they want solved, a need that must be met or a result that is desired. So at this stage, it should be your client's needs that you talk about, regardless if it's in an advertisement, a Facebook post or in a phone call. For example, instead of saying that I sell business coaching, I could say that I help business owners get more customers or earn more money.

Phase Two:
Like

When you've caught your future clients' attention, it's obvious they must like you or what you have to offer. They typically do that when you communicate in their own language and use pictures or examples they can relate to.

If you have a physical shop, it's about the location and your window facing the street. If you speak to someone, you can tell them about similar clients you've helped in the past. If you're communicating online, you can refer to your homepage, where they can get relevant information through blog posts (video, sound or text) or by getting an eBook, a discount coupon or a template when they sign up for your newsletter. Phases 1 and 2 happen quickly one after the other, and they require you to be precise in your communication. In this way, your clients will feel as though you are talking directly to them. As mentioned earlier, we're living in a click-paced culture and you only have a couple of seconds to catch their attention online – and perhaps a couple of minutes if you talk directly with them.

There will always be others on the market with similar offerings; the key is to know that people buy from people, and if you want to inspire trust and get people to like you,

you have to be yourself. Having a common thread across all your business communications will help you appear authentic and naturally attract clients you like and who'll like you. If clients buy something from you, recommend you or help you, they do so because they like you and what you do, and they trust you. Therefore, the best you can do is be honest and be yourself.

Remarkable women, such as Linse Kessler, Soulaima Gourani and Michelle Hviid are controversial and opinionated. They have had the odds stacked against them, from brain tumors to growing up in bars and ghettos and raising their children alone. They are now successful influencers, very proactive and with a positive take on life. Each of them has, in her own way, created a solid livelihood by, among other things, speaking honestly. Their followers love them and are very loyal, which creates the foundation for a good business.

When you show who you are, you must show what's relevant for your clients. If you're selling to companies, typically it'll be your professionalism and your professional values that are important, as well as how you work, while your private life will occupy a much smaller place. For example, I adore skiing and was part of the national youth team when I was a teenager, but this isn't something I mention in my communication, as it adds no value in terms of my being a mother and self-employed entrepreneur.

Last, but not least, it's far easier to communicate as yourself, and if you enjoy the freedom of being self-employed, you'll also love the freedom of being yourself. I've tried both, and it unleashes the most amazing energy when you earn money on 'just' being you and doing what you have a passion for.

Phase Three: Trust

This phase can last from five minutes to over a year, depending on what you're selling. If it's ball pens, it doesn't take long. In this case, trust can easily be established by offering a full refund or a providing your products with a guarantee. If, on the other hand, you're selling an expensive item, or something that requires your client investing a lot of time, then it'll take longer to establish the required trust. Trust can be in you as a person, in your business, or in the product you're offering. I often call the trust phase the uncertainty phase, because at this level you invest a lot in creating trust and building relationships with your potential customers, but it can feel uncertain as it takes time before you see any results.

Even with good tips, don't be fooled by what others write on the web about getting immediate results.

TRUST TIP NO.1:
YOU SELL MORE WITH NEWSLETTERS

This is true because you can write directly to people in their inbox. The time and the price for writing the email is the same, whether your newsletter has one or 100,000 readers.

The key to writing a good newsletter is writing one that sells and having enough subscribers. Even though 100 may seem a lot to begin with, and you must usually have thousands before you see a real effect, but that depends, of course, on what you're selling. To get more subscribers, you need to get more visitors to your website, for example through paid ads or from other people linking to your site.

TRUST TIP NO. 2:
YOU NEED A 'PROPER' HOMEPAGE

Yes, because everybody will start by Googling you. But what is often overlooked is that people quickly click away again. You have to find a way to communicate with your (potential) clients or create enough visitors to your home-page so that the majority who visit stay on to explore your business offerings.

TRUST TIP NO. 3:
YOU SHOULD ATTEND TRADE FAIRS

Yes, that leads to getting contacts, and it's nice being visible in relevant trade fairs.

But if you don't follow it up afterwards and maintain the relationship, you'll be forgotten in no time.

These tips are helpful and work, but they are not enough unless they are part of a coherent strategy. It's important you see the whole picture and have a common thread in all you do, so you get the most out of your work efforts.

Ask yourself the following questions:
- Where do I want to be visible, and to whom?
- How do I want to communicate?
- What is my message?

Birgitte Feldborg was the mother of five and in her mid-forties when she became self-employed in 2010. She hadn't learned about sales and marketing before that, or defined a specific target group, so she had to learn it by herself the hard way.

Before becoming self-employed, Birgitte had been chief purchasing and logistics officer at a firm where she was required to travel 120 days a year. It was hard enough with four children, but manageable because her ex-husband helped look after their children every other week. When she got remarried and got pregnant with her fifth child, it was different. By that time she wasn't too fond of her job, so she was ready for something different.

Birgitte had long cherished a dream of becoming self-employed, and in 2008 Andreas was born – when the financial crisis began – and the firm Birgitte was working for went bankrupt while she was on maternity leave. It was the perfect time to try something new. She signed up for a course on entrepreneur.now, and planned to earn a living from doing bookkeeping for smaller companies and taking on various HR assignments. The latter she had to quit, though, because due to the crisis, that was the first area that businesses cut down on.

"I had a traditional approach to starting up. I had an office at home, I had business cards and a homepage made, and I put a little ad in the newspaper. Then I waited. To my great surprise, nothing happened! I chanced upon an acquaintance who invited me to a network meeting. There I made my first sales pitch, which I hated, and as my friend so bluntly put it: 'That sure as hell didn't sell you.'

"I heeded her words, and at the next network meeting I attended, I'd written something down so I knew what to say. That was the way I managed to get my first clients.

"All along, the plan was that bookkeeping would help me get started, and then I'd leave that. When I was contacted by Lene, who was responsible for the entrepreneurs course I had taken, she asked me if I wanted to teach accountancy and administration as part of the study. I had no doubts, and said yes on the spot. I like helping people who have passion and take responsibility for what they do. Though I wasn't earning a huge amount, it has improved my quality of life, and when I look at the family's overall finances, everything is in order now."

As she went along, Birgitte also stumbled upon stories on how to earn easy money.

"Providing an online course, can earn you a passive income. It might become a supplement, but it's really an uphill battle making a living from it. Your clients also get a hundred times more out of participating live than in online courses. My experience is that people have to know you for a while before they buy anything. It requires a consistent effort to create relationships and trust, independently of how you want to sell. Online is not enough in itself; you must also interact with your clients. The most important thing must be finding out who your clients are. It's difficult getting to the heart of it, and it's often under-prioritized, or made far too complicated, with personas and smart marketing expressions."

Luckily, there are many ways you can create trust and expedite the purchase process. Naturally, you must show what a difference your product, or your service, will make for your clients. The quicker and easier you demonstrate that what you're offering gives the clients the results they want, the less they'll focus on the price.

Client feedback is particularly good; this will provide proof and is more credible, since it's other people recommending you. If you have before-and-after pictures, that's also powerful, as your clients can see the result. If you can't get pictures, in your text ask one of your clients to provide a before-and -after story.

You shouldn't be afraid of giving something out for free in the beginning. If you're selling physical products, it can be samples. If you're offering some kind of counselling, then share as much of your knowledge as you can and combine several platforms like social media posts, blogs, lectures and webinars. This way, you showcase both who you are as a person, and your professionalism.

Besides creating trust in you, in your business and in your product, sometimes you also have to help your client gain confidence in themselves. For example, if you're selling a coaching course, a weight-loss diet course or a training program, you must show how your clients will be supported all the way to achieve the desired result and that their money is not wasted.

A very effective method to build trust and a shortcut to more clients is through cooperation partners. A cooperation partner is a business that ideally is bigger than yours and targets the same group as you, but isn't a competitor. If you're selling physical products, it can be a distributor that ensures your goods get out to more shops. If you're offering your knowledge, it can be companies that want you to hold lectures or courses for their clients. The advantages of having a cooperation partner are that you reach out to more people, and at the same time, you build up trust and credibility quicker.

When I had my second business, I sold management development and coaching to day care centers. I quickly got fed up with contacting them one by one, and therefore I started a collaboration with a Day Care Centre Confederation that then recommended me. With Mors Business, I've established many such collaborations, DANA being one.

DANA is the self-employed community's unemployment insurance fund, and thus I get exposure to their 25,000 members and they get access to lots of my knowledge through events and online activities. It's a win-win situation.

Think about the following questions:
- Who could you cooperate with?
- What companies target the same group as you?
- What value can you create for the companies?
- What value can you, together, give to your clients?

Phase Four: Buy

Trust and relationships are seldom enough to get clients. It's also important to meet with clients and personally encourage them to buy your offering 'now'. Most decisions can be postponed, so if you don't help your clients make the decision now, they'll wait or something will get in the way, and they won't end up becoming a client. You can use several triggers from everyday life to provoke action on your clients' part:

- Limited amounts make the product appear rare and create the conditions for people to hurry, before it's too late.
- Deadlines work well to stimulate your clients to buy now, instead of waiting. It can be sales or promotions.
- You can also offer the option to pay in instalments so the cost doesn't overwhelm them.
- Awarding bonuses to your clients will make them feel that they are getting value for their money and these will also create a loyal relationship.

Once I held a webinar that several hundred people signed up for. I'd written about it in advance on my newsletter and on numerous Facebook posts. The day before, I did send a last reminder to remind people to sign up, and an additional 100 people did so. So, even when you use triggers, your clients often have to hear the message many times before making their minds up.

For this reason, sales campaigns are an effective tool to selling. During the sales campaign, you can address all concerns and at the same time show your clients what your product can do for them.

What your sales campaign looks like depends on who your target group is and what you're selling. If your clients are companies, a campaign could look like this:

1. Make contact with an initial phone call and agree to meet in person.
2. Develop the relationship and build trust, hold one or more meetings where you get to know each other and you find out what their needs are.
3. Sell your product/services by making an offer based on your conversations and follow up until they sign the purchase order.

The last point is critical and it's your job to maintain contact, and the whole time agree upon the next step; what's to happen, and when. Many forget to follow up and just sit and wait for the companies to come back to them. But this seldom happens. You have to have a plan for selling so new clients stream in on a regular basis; otherwise, you'll experience a roller coaster in your business, where at times it's very busy, and at other times there's no money coming in.

If you're running your campaign online, it can be set up like this:

1. Make contact, start with ads that attract the reader to your homepage where they can; for example, sign up for a webinar or an ebook.

2. Build up the relationship and the trust, then send a series of emails containing cases and addressing objections your clients might have towards what you're offering. What you write will show your client the value your product creates or the difference it makes.
3. Sell by making an offer with a deadline and use several triggers. You can definitely send several emails where you mention the deadline, preferably at the end of the email as a PS, which most often gets read, and perhaps also on the subject line on the last email. Remember to vary the rest of the text in your emails, so you don't bore your readers.

If you have a physical shop, the campaign can start with ads on social media and the local newspapers and run a period with sales, or make it known that a new, limited collection has come in. You can run the campaigns several times a year and thus influence your sales.

Connect
the Dots

Now you have the four phases for your strategy. With your target group as a starting point, and with sales as a goal, you can now choose which elements you want to use in your business. It's important that you also check if the strategy matches you and your personality. You can be equally successful if you choose one method or the other, so choose one you want to act upon and work from on a daily basis. If sales and marketing fill 50–80 percent of your working time, what do you feel most like doing? Being in a shop, being online, talking on the phone and meeting people, holding lectures … ?

It's important you consider the following:

- Where, and how, should your clients hear about you/your product/your business?
- What can you offer for them to like you/your product/your business?
- How will you build relationships and create trust?
- What will you do to make your clients buy immediately?
- What sales campaigns can you make?
- Whom can you cooperate with?

It can take some time to figure it out, and it can change the way you and your business develop. For example, I started doing a lot of online marketing and phone counselling when I started Mors Business, because my twins were young, I was tired, and I wanted to work from home. Now that they're older and sleep through the night, I'd rather be out networking.

Connecting Strategy, Phases and Revenue Goals

The phases in your strategy can now be connected to the revenue goals set at the beginning of this step. If we stick to the example of wanting to earning £50,000, then it's not really enough to know that you're going to sell 1,000 one-to-one sessions, 15 seats on a course or sell 2,000 eBooks. You must also know what sales and marketing effort is required to sell that much.

Let's say this is the first course you're holding. There are only 15 seats for sale, but on the flip side, the price is rather steep (£3,333). Therefore, it wouldn't be unrealistic if you started your sales campaign six months in advance. The campaign could look like this:

- Phase 1–2 'know' and 'like': 10 Facebook-ads to be made with text and photos, and a budget of £1,000.
- Phase 3 'trust': 15 emails to send to interested people who are on your list, or who have clicked an ad and signed up for a webinar or a lecture.
- Phase 4 'sale': 5 webinars and 5 lectures or info evenings where you sell the seats and get to answer whatever questions the participants may have before buying a seat.

- Partnerships with other businesses that target the same group and that would like to tell them about your course. Perhaps also affiliate partners that get a share of the sale if they get someone to sign up for your course.

If it's the first time, the campaign, the preparations for the course and materials can take six months of your working time – perhaps even more.

Consider what you can do in a tangible way in the different phases so your clients get enough knowledge about what you're offering and can make a decision on buying it.

Retain their attention and solve problems

It's not always enough to get noticed by new clients; it's equally important to retain your clients' attention. You know how it is with fitness centers: you sign up in January, filled with good intentions, then it's Monday again and you don't use your membership. Fitness centers earn good money on the clients' lacking willpower and self-discipline, but for most businesses, this would be a problem.

Depending on your industry, it is very important to make sure that there's a good experience right after the purchase. Some go about it by sending a 'congratulations on your new purchase' email or a generic welcome email, while others make sure there's a personal follow up a couple of days later.

Statistics from Lee Resources Inc. show that only 4% of disgruntled customers complain; the remaining 96% go over to the competition. The interesting and surprising thing about the survey was that it showed that a client who goes from being disgruntled to being satisfied because the company solved their complaint tells 12 other people. That means that one client you've solved a problem for in a good way – even if there was something wrong with your product – will be more loyal and recommend you more than a client who's just pleased. Therefore, errors or defects in what you're offering don't necessarily have to be bad for your business, as long as you deal with it properly, and focus on the client's experience.

Test the Ideas Early on in the Process

The time it takes before your strategy starts yielding results, and the effort you have to put in, depends both on the quality of your product and the size of your existing client base. If you've already got many satisfied clients, it'll be quicker and easier to launch and sell a new product than for a business that has recently been set up.

Birgitte Feldborg worked towards launching a new product on the entrepreneur.now website. "We produced a great and detailed online course that demonstrated how to create your own homepage," she says. "But we were not having much luck in selling it. Then, through our networking activities, we came across four people who needed a new homepage each. Despite having taken the course, they all felt that it was too difficult to do the technical parts on their own."

"We revised the product, and provided half of what was to be learned online, and the other half was taught through personal guidance. Again, it was no easy process, because our dream was to make something that was 100 % online to achieve more flexibility, so the question was whether we had the time and the inclination to redo the concept, or if we should abandon it altogether. If we had tested the concept earlier and known that it couldn't be sold as a pure online course, we could have abandoned it."

When the sisters Jane and Nanna Ulsøe started Canvas Planner in 2014, they had a crystal-clear mission: "We wanted to help people work in a smarter way. When you work with others, there are far too many distractions from emails, meetings and follow ups," Jane says. "Therefore, we developed software that gives teams a common visual starting point, so that in the blink of an eye they can see who's doing what, and then they can more easily work in the same direction. We differ from other tech companies in that we have no tech background. We're both project managers, and together we've developed a product that we both felt was missing in our working lives."

Canvas Planner is an online tool that gives businesses and their teams a visual overview of mutual projects, and thus makes it easier to collaborate. To begin with, nobody thought about or saw the need for visual software to be used in management tasks, so they quickly abandoned the thought of finding investors and 'bootstrapped' (they paid for the development of their software themselves).

"We didn't have a lot of money when we first started the business, and so most of the banks that we approached wanted our parents to act as guarantors, but we didn't want that. Instead of wasting our time with big banks in big cities, we chose to pitch to smaller banks further afield. They were very enthusiastic, and finally we reached an agreement with one of them for a bank overdraft. We couldn't afford developers in Denmark. Instead, we had a prototype made in Pakistan, through one of Nanna's contacts.

"There were challenges with the development part of the process. The developers weren't up to scratch, and there were some cultural problems, so the software was coded in the wrong language, which would never work, because it was too laborious. We wasted a whole year on it, and it almost put us totally off entirely." Jane at the time had primarily a supporting function. She bought a share in the business so they could get some better developers on board.

"We found developers in Denmark, who were able to redesign our software at a reasonable price. Luckily, not all the work on the prototype was wasted, and the developers were able to make the next version much better," Jane recalls.

Despite having wasted a year on development in Pakistan, the two sisters quickly got back on their feet. In 2015, they developed a new version and got the first paying clients in 2016. Among other things, that's due to their willingness to adapt and being good at focusing on what's best for the business.

As a 'lean start-up', Jane and Nanna had asked the users right from the start what their needs and challenges were, and Jane stresses the importance of this. "It's hugely important to test an idea from the start. If an idea is to die, it must die quickly, so you don't waste too many resources on it. Your closest friends and relatives will mostly give positive feedback, so in our case we used an advisory board made up of people from our target group.

"So, I would always advise to get out and meet people from your target group, and people who can help you with your business, so you have the right advice.

"There will be many things you won't know before you start, so it's difficult to make a perfectly clear plan. You must be willing to adapt and make it up as you go along. With time, we've become even more familiar with our product. You must have a good amount of optimism, confidence in it and not develop any doubts when things are tough. It's a good thing we weren't alone; we have been there to pull each other up in difficult times," Jane Ulsøe believes.

Instead of looking for money for expensive marketing campaigns, Nanna and Jane chose to do a silent launch, where they sneak their product onto the market via direct sales.

"It's difficult to sell a new product when you haven't established any clients. It's said that the first ten clients are the hardest. That's why we prefer to actively market Canvas Planner when we have a number of paying clients, so we can use them as reference. By doing a silent launch, we can find out how people use the product, and which industries are most interested, so it's easier to market afterwards. At the moment, our clients list includes approximately 60 companies and 2,000 registered users, and new users are being added every day. We expect to launch and do active marketing in the course in the fall of 2017," Jane says.

Choose a Strategy That You Love

Another influential factor for success is whether you stay within the industry you have experience in, or if you've chosen something different altogether, because you want to try something new. I meet many women who are tired of their jobs and who take courses in coaching, therapy, massage, nutrition, etc. and want to turn it into their livelihood. It's often an uphill battle, because they lack enough experience in the field to charge the kind of prices they would need to be charging clients to get the income they could live off and create enough credibility in relation to their experience. The advantages of staying in the industry you've worked in before are plenty. You would already have a network of people you can sell to or team up with and you have so much experience you can charge sensible prices for your work.

It would also have been much easier for me, from a purely business point of view, to continue with recruiting instead of starting all over again with Mors Business. But it was a conscious choice that my working life was going to be different, and from the very start, I was aware that it'd take longer before I'd have an income that matched what I could earn as a recruitment consultant.

I know self-employed women who stayed within their field and earn over £10,000 a month who are disappointed, because it's no longer their passion, but they don't dare take the plunge into what they really have a passion for, due to the fear of losing too much money. I also know some women who earn £1,500 a month and are very happy, because they have the freedom they'd dreamt of, they are following their heart and they have time for their family. There are also those who succeed, who hit the nail on the head the first time and earn a lot of money with their passion. My point is that there are no ready-made answers and no guarantees. Therefore, the business and strategy you choose must, above all, make you happy. You must be true to yourself, your vision and your goals.

Stick to Your Values as Your Business Grows

In January 2006, Anja Lytzen started the online toy company Lirum Larum Leg. At the time, she had no idea that four years later she'd be named the female entrepreneur of the year and win the e-commerce prize for small businesses.

Anja had played with the thought of becoming self-employed for about a year and had considered opening a shop selling children's wear with a friend, but she couldn't see how they would earn enough to get two salaries from the business. Also, she couldn't quite see how everyday life would function together with family life. At the time, she was working at her parents' ice cream shop, and she had just had her second child.

"I settled for toys, because I had two young children and felt comfortable in that world. I'd also tried buying something online and had had an insipid experience, with a dull website and a bland packaging of the product. 'I'm sure I can do better than that,' I thought. There already existed good specialized toy shops that dealt in quality toys, but they weren't particularly accessible. My vision was to create the experience of entering an old-fashioned toy shop – only online, and thus accessible to all. My online shop would radiate quality and design, and clients would be mothers like myself who wanted gorgeous toys that were different for their children," Anja says.

Anja spent every evening researching and was well prepared the first time she went off to a toy fair.

"I bought products based on what I'd buy for my own children. There wasn't much analysis behind it other than my instinct and recommendations and suggestions from the parents in my network."

Before Anja launched the firm on 20 April 2006, she did a lot of preparations. "I established a cooperation with a gifted graphic designer, and the logo – the giraffe – was drawn. The name, Lirum Larum Leg, taken from the chorus of 'Jens Hansens bondegård' ('Ol' MacDonald Had a Farm'), came about as one of the first things in February 2006, after having brainstormed for two days, by checking out old children's books and nursery rhymes.

"I'd saved £25,000, which I spent on designing the site and buying my first products. My mother still had her ice cream shop, and she let me set up my shop there, in the cellar, without having to pay rent. It really wasn't a big, shiny solution, but it was enough for me to get me started because I wanted to start cautiously in every way." Anja recalls.

Anja was very much aware of her strengths and weaknesses, thus she was not afraid of investing in help with the tasks she couldn't handle herself.

"The first person I ever contacted was a graphic designer. If the purchase experience in my shop was to be good, it had to be enjoyable, functional and different, so there was no point in being stingy there. I had no prerequisites to create a website from scratch, but I looked at a number of other sites and considered what would work for me."

The marketing budget was small and only covered a few small ads in the paper. In those days, there was no social media to help businesses get started, but Anja had asked everyone in her network for their email address, so she could write to them when the homepage was ready.

"On the very first day, ten orders came in. It was crazy. On the second day, I couldn't recognize some of the names on the new orders. I realized that people I knew had started a wave of publicity for me as they shared my email on to others in their networks. I'm positive it paved the way for my immediate success, which to me confirmed that my website was good, and that people were happy to recommend it to others," Anja says.

Anja also tried spreading the news on other fronts. "I worked in a very targeted manner to get publicity in the press, and I was lucky. We were mentioned in big Danish newspapers like *Børsen*, *Jyllands-Posten* and the local press, and it wasn't just a matter of sending out a press release and hoping for the best. I followed it up once, twice, three times, until we established a dialogue. According to one of my friends, my motto must be that behind every 'no' there's a silent 'yes', and that I feel that is true. Getting PR is not as hard as many believe it to be."

In the cellar under her mother's ice cream shop, the stock of toys grew and soon there was room for no more. "The money I got from sales was reinvested in new products straight away. In September, the shortage of space was obvious and new orders came in all the time. I had to leave home," Anja says.

From the beginning, Anja had agreed with her mother that if and when she got too busy to keep up with Lirum Larum Leg, her mother was to sell her ice cream shop and join her. She did so in December 2006, and it wasn't a moment too soon. "I'd always thought I was busy, but when Christmas shopping was upon us, it was totally insane, the amount of orders almost knocked the wind out of us."

"After the first Christmas, I incorporated the stock management into the shop solution for sales to function at their optimum. It lifted some of the admin burden, but there was still a lot of admin work that wasn't fun at all and took a lot of my time."

It was Anja's father who took over the task. And she explains: "Finance doesn't interest me that much, as long as I know how things are going in general terms. But we've grown with time, and I've been forced to make myself take an interest in it, because strategic decisions have to be made, as all of a sudden this is a big gamble."

The range of products has also grown from 500 to many thousands, and Anja has hired a number of employees to manage the stock, orders and customer service. The first year, 6,000 parcels were sent off, and the following year the number had doubled to 12,000. The first busy Christmas shopping season taught Anja it was necessary to have more efficient stock management.

"It was a whirlwind, but we didn't overextend our finances. The whole time we've been in control, and I believe that's one of the reasons we've maintained our success. Some people have asked us how we've experienced growth without major investment in marketing; we know that it is our constant focus on service and quality that are our trademarks for success."

Anja makes sure her clients are satisfied by sending follow-up emails to customers when they order something. She reports that 95% of the clients would buy again, and that 95% would recommend her business to others.

"We have social media now, which makes it easier to spread the word, but at the same time, they require you to be willing to adapt and keep up. We send out a newsletter, which is a great tool, and a good way to tell customers about new products. Every time we stock a new toy,

I truly look forward to informing our customers about it," Anja says. "I'm still thrilled about my products. Competition has become significantly tougher. Everyone can make a nice homepage and deliver quickly, so in that aspect we don't stand out as much as we did. I have to be ahead of the game in terms of stock and trends, and I attend international trade fairs in both the spring and fall, among other events, to keep up."

One would think it's cheaper running an online store than a physical one, but such a large warehouse entails many expenses.

"We have exactly the same expenses as a traditional shop, perhaps more, because I also pay rent, and I have to pay people to pack the products the client has ordered. The shipping bill alone is astronomical," Anja says, and that's why it makes good sense that Anja chooses quality instead of cheap prices, as she wouldn't be able to compete in this way.

"I won't compromise on quality, and I listen to my gut. Ultimately, we like to make children and parents happy. We always put a real effort into wrapping the toy in beautiful wrapping paper, so one can proudly pass the gift on," Anja says.

Quality is something many parents appreciate, and in 2015, Anja and Lirum Larum Leg won an award for the 'Best Toy Shop'.

The target group, which in the beginning was mothers like Anja – ages 20–45 – has also changed as more and more learn how to use the net, like grandparents, for example.

"In 2013, we needed more help with administration, a new IT system, and more space. I reinvested what I'd earned, and from August 2014 to August 2015 was pretty wild for us, because we implemented a new IT system and moved to larger premises. At the same time, we got in a number of new brands and focused more on interior products, which are a large part of our growth."

"Even if the process has been hard, it's all been worth it. It's been crucial for me to stick to our goal and values and grow from there. So, it's been a great pleasure to experience our success without making any sacrifices. Those who've told me at times that you can't run a business with your heart are wrong. Lirum Larum Leg is living proof that you can put your heart in what you do – and still run a sensible business."

The turnover has topped several millions, the business grew 25% in 2016, with 14 full-time employees, which is increased to approximately 50 around the Christmas season.

Textbook theories and strategies that worked yesterday don't necessarily still work. When it comes down to it, it's your business, your responsibility and your life, so when making decisions, make sure you can live with the consequences, be they good or bad. In the third and last step, you get help with optimizing your resources, so you can achieve more and free up enough time for your business and your family.

STEP 3

Optimize Your Resources and Attain More

Prioritize

People often ask me how it's possible to be self-employed and the mother of young children. Is it possible at all? Surely, I must either be a bad mother, meaning I don't see enough of my children, or I must be a non-committed business woman, because the business is not my top priority. But being self-employed is a lifestyle where your personal and your professional life are intertwined. It's a delicate balance that requires you to be very stern in prioritizing. I haven't met a self-employed mother who hasn't eliminated many things in order to succeed professionally and lead a happy family life. But it really can be done. And your life can still be awesome, because what you choose to do is what means most to you.

It can be hard eliminating things. Sometimes it might feel impossible if you've been doing the same things year in, year out, or if you have a pleaser gene, or if you're optimistic in terms of the time you have available.

Often, it's external causes that make us stop and change our priorities. That was the case for one of my clients. She was pressed for time between work, time for her friends, her boyfriend and her young son, and she had the clear feeling there was nothing she could eliminate. Then suddenly her son fell ill and had to be hospitalized for some time. In the blink of an eye, she cleared her calendar so she could be with him. When he recovered and could go home again, she was crystal clear about her priorities and decided to change her planning, which, as she says, has only made her life better.

I myself have radically cut down on dinners with friends, stopped spending time in front of the TV and lowered my expectations on how much I'll take part in school events. They're pleasant things, but they steal time from my children and my business. That doesn't mean that I don't see my friends, but it's less than before. I make sure I finish evening appointments early and go home so I can get enough sleep to be fresh when the children wake up early the next day. For the same reason, I totally stopped drinking alcohol, as it affected my sleep.

Now, I'm not saying that you should eliminate the same things as I have, but you do need to prioritize and cut down or drop some of your activities. The best way to do this is by determining which activities give you good energy, and which make you too tired in the long run.

You have to be an adult and be reasonable. You know that in the long run it's the wise and sensible choices that will give you the results you want. In this instance, your vision is an important tool, as it reminds you why you're doing what you're doing and what result you're hoping for. The vision, and the life you make for yourself, should be more enriching and rewarding than the things you're relinquishing.

Exercise: This Is How You Prioritize Your Tasks

If you find it hard to prioritize the important things over fun things or old habits, you can do this:

1. Sit down and think about your vision and look at what's important for you. Imagine how it will feel when the vision turns into reality.

2. When you feel the drive and the desire to bring it to fruition, grab your calendar and set aside time for the important things; typically, you should allocate 90% of your time to work and family and 10% to friends and exercise.

3. If there's still room in the calendar for more activities, those are the times when you can watch TV or say yes to things that aren't part of the vision.

4. Start each day looking at your vision, and feel it, so you motivate yourself to act upon what's important for it to become a reality.

Babies, Maternity Leave and Business

When you have children, it can be hard to make ends meet. If business is good, many women prefer to pay for their maternity leave themselves so they can work a bit and keep the wheels turning while still having time to enjoy their baby. Precisely because they're their own boss, no one will look at them the wrong way if they show up late, take nursing breaks, or work evenings. Creative, flexible solutions are possible, where work and maternity leave interflow. For many passionate women, it's also best to keep on working instead of putting things on hold during the length of their maternity leave.

Anna Bogdanova has just had her second child, Sylvester, who's six months old as I write. She talks about this period: "I stepped away for four weeks before the birth because my business partner, Louise, insisted I do so. It was a nice and liberating feeling to know that someone I could rely on was running the business in my absence. But, after a month of maternity leave, I couldn't stay away any longer and went back to work. Nowadays, I rarely work at night, only when we've put the children to bed. That's the smart thing about being online; I don't have to look presentable and refreshed at a specific hour."

Pernille Birkenfeldt has been her own boss since 2013; she offers services that help self-employed people with their finances. While I'm writing this book, she's on maternity leave with her first child, Malou.

"I discussed the finances with my boyfriend and read up on the maternity leave rules. For the time being, my homepage is on standby, so nobody is buying my online courses right now. I'm holding six months full-time maternity leave, and then I'll be starting back part-time. Financially speaking, that will mean that I'm starting my business back from scratch, which does worry me," Pernille says.

Apart from the financial aspect, Pernille has also gained a new perspective on life after becoming a mother. "At the moment, I spend time thinking about the future. I've discovered you don't get that much done when you're on maternity leave. Now this is the first time, so I've been a bit too optimistic. It's all very new. I've come to realize how hard it is to make everyday life function with children and work, and I have great respect for couples where both are full-time employed and at the same time look after the family."

Even though the financial aspect can be challenging, being self-employed does have its perks, Pernille says: "I was so grateful to be self-employed during my pregnancy, because I was so tired. It was nice taking it easy, adapting my work and looking after myself. I haven't been particularly good at that in the past. I've had to revise my prejudice around how long one should stay home and accept that I'm 'one of those' who sends her six-month-old daughter to the nursery. But I also know that I'm a better mother and have more energy."

"I've had to work with my view of myself, and that there's nothing wrong with me as a mother, because I also feel like working. In this respect, it's great that others in my network are self-employed and have young children as well. It means a lot that we understand one another.

"It's hard being on maternity leave when you want to be doing everything at work. It sounds like a contradiction saying no, or asking clients to wait. I feel torn. But it's great to take a break and be forced to live in the here and now and have the opportunity to enjoy spending time with my daughter. I also need to be my 'old self' and have 'me' time – just a couple of hours on my own. Then I have more to give. It really is the same thing when you're working. You have to remember to top yourself up, so you have more to give to the clients."

The Dilemma

When you're passionate about your work, and your business develops in an exciting direction, it can be hard not to work, even if you love your children. It's not always easy finding a balance where both children and business get the attention they deserve.

When Anna Bogdanova had her first son, Valentin, she was at that time tied to the self-employed hamster wheel. She was offering one-to-one classes, which meant that she was relying on selling her time on an hourly basis, which is difficult when you have a baby to look after.

"The first maternity year in particular was really hard. I thought I could have two weeks' maternity leave and get right back to work. I had trouble accepting that I couldn't, and that made it even worse. I had to cancel many one-to-one classes, because Valentin was sick or just wanted his mother. I tried to push through it, but ended up collapsing," Anna says.

The dilemma and the frustrations of trying to combine work and motherhood affects many people. Jane Ulsøe from Canvas Planner expresses the guilty conscience that at times rears its ugly head: "I sometimes get haunted by my guilty conscience. I work from home, and now the children are so big that they come home alone and play with their friends when I'm there. I feel it's nice for them that I'm there; but on the other hand, it's challenging for me to stop work, because there's always something I can be doing. I ensure that I am mentally present for my family by clearly defining the times that I work so my family knows when I'm available. It can be irritating if they're waiting for me and don't know when I'm done. It's a question of practice. I have to learn to stop and be present in my interaction with my children."

Everyday tasks can get cumbersome, even if you have the freedom to do your own planning and you are the only boss. It's a matter of realizing that there are several ways of being with your children and giving them closeness and experiences. We're often stuck in a rut as to how society expects us to act as employees, and it can be a bit of a job finding a rhythm that works for you and your family.

Camilla Mengers had success from the start with Albi's Kaffebar. She had to take the good with the bad when getting used to her new lifestyle and to other ways of being with her children, Alberte and Mingus.

"My husband and I opened the café in June and worked every day for the first three months. By September, we felt we needed a break and introduced a weekly day off, which after a year led up to us closing Mondays and Tuesdays. We spend the two days with the children once they come home from school." Camilla says. The family lives above the café so no time is wasted travelling to and from work, but it also comes with its challenges: "It can be hard separating work and days off, when they're both the same place, and every now and then I end up working on my days off."

There are no summer holidays, as the city they are situated in is a holiday destination, and that's when a large proportion of their revenue is generated. So, they go to the beach in the evening and enjoy time as a family around that.

"In the summer I start at 4.15am and close at 5pm, both weekdays and weekends. In the winter, we can open at 6.30am. We have no days off during the school break. The children are here, they go to their club, spend a week's holiday at my mother's or my father's sister in England. We involve the children, so that they feel that the café belongs to all of us. We've ask the children to share their ideas so they have made suggestions like decoration (so children also feel welcome) and having hot cocoa with marshmallows was also their idea. The café is named after Alberte, whose nickname is Albi. Mingus is represented by a chocolate muffin, and the town's children know there's a 'Mingo muffin'," Camilla says.

"If we're busy when the children come home, it's my mother or mother-in-law who looks after them and makes them something to eat. Since having opened the café, I have missed spending as much time with the children. It was really hard for the children and for me to come to terms with my not being able to be there for them the moment they needed me.

"The weekends are particularly hard for me, because we can never see the children's soccer games. I feel strongly that time with the children now is important. In five years' time, they'll be too big, and they won't feel like being with us in the same way anymore. For that reason, we've decided that after September we'll close on Sundays in the winter, so we can spend more time with the children and watch them doing sports."

The success has given Camilla and her husband some opportunities they didn't have previously. "After a very busy year and a half, we felt that we needed some family time, so we closed the café throughout the whole of January, and spent a month in Thailand. We also had two weeks' holiday in September two years running. These trips are the carrot for the children and for us. In addition, we also enjoy the small moments we have as a couple that we never used to have, because we had different jobs and both worked long hours. Now, sometimes we have a quiet morning where we sit in the garden and enjoy the sun with a nice cup of coffee."

There have been mixed reactions to their new lifestyle from people around thems, and on this Camilla says: "We've had to relinquish a lot in the beginning, and we've often upset family members because we haven't been able to go to birthdays, confirmations and other events on weekends.

"We try to see our friends in the evening, because it's important, but we pay the price when we get up and go to work next day. We bring in too much on Sundays to close that day. Having said that, I definitely don't regret having taken the plunge, because in the end we get so much more than what we've relinquished."

The Children's Perspective

Some good advice, which was given to me from another self-employed mother, was to drop the guilty conscience when I'm not with my children. "Your children don't miss you any less when you have a guilty conscience." If you're doing something, enjoy it, and tell your children why it's important that you do it. Then when you're with your children, you can show them how important they are to you. Your children learn that you have to work for what you want, but also that your dreams can come true, which is important knowledge for them for when they want to live out their own dreams.

One of the concerns I often see among women who are, or want to become self-employed is that they're afraid of how it will affect their children. Will the children blame them later?

We all want to give our children a good childhood and prepare them for a good life as adults, and no matter what we do, there'll certainly be decisions your children will thank you for, and things they'll probably do differently when they have their own children. When you ask adults or older children with self-employed mothers what they think about their mother's work, the response is often very positive.

Pia Nissen Tylak's mother was self-employed, which meant she had rather different working hours. "She worked for a dental technician and quit to become a self-employed foot therapist. Later on, she expanded into facial treatments, a clinic, and finally a training centre with my stepfather. She never advertised, but she always had waiting lists. I think it was because she was interested, instead of wanting to be interesting. I've always been very proud of my mother. She's a gift to mankind with her positive way of being. I learned early on to take more responsibility because she had unsociable working hours. It taught me to find solutions for things on my own, but I've never doubted her love, and I've always felt loved."

Anja Lytzen also inherited her interest. Her parents had a yarn shop, and they also owned a mail order firm. They started in the late 1970s, at a time when it was modern to do your own knitting. In the late 1980s, when home knitting was no longer trendy, Anja's parents closed down their mail order firm and changed course. They converted their premises and opened an ice cream and chocolate shop.

"I remember helping in the yarn shop as a child. I've definitely been influenced by their work ethic and this upbringing. They had a gene that drove them. As an entrepreneur, you don't give up. You fight!" Anja says.

Timing

Life with children is ever-changing. There are phases in their lives where they're super easy, and others where they demand a lot of time and attention from you. Sometimes, when you've just found a rhythm, and you think everything's fine, it changes again. On the other hand, everything might seem hopeless, and then suddenly everything falls into place on its own. The same applies to your business. As you can read about Pernille, Camilla and Anna, the different phases have advantages and disadvantages, and it's about making the most out of the circumstances and enjoying the other possibilities of being self-employed.

Louise from MyMonii got pregnant in the middle of the starting phase, while they were in the process of finding investors and doing product development. "I was wildly in love with my boyfriend, Jens, and felt I was ready to have children. I said so to Jens, and he was immediately on board. It's important for me to have children while I can, so I'll find a way of sorting out the business, I thought.

"I got pregnant in February 2016, and I was terribly nervous about telling that to my partner and Business Angel,

Thor, and Jonas, with whom I work every day. I didn't have the courage, and many times I almost did, but held back. When I finally said it, Thor was so happy and touched. He's a father himself, and thought it was wild and fantastic and gave me a huge hug. Jonas did the same. "However, when things went wrong with the investors, I did feel the pregnancy was a huge obstacle. I was really backed up by my boyfriend, Jens, who said we'd work it out. He took it easy, and was very reassuring. He just said: 'Let's calculate how long we can manage without you getting paid and take it from there.' Support from my base was an important contributing factor to my keeping at it, and believing we'd make it.

"I had a good pregnancy. I was well and energetic, which I'm grateful for. I worked over my due time and held courses over my due time. I'd told people what the lay of the land was, and they were ok with that," Louise Ferslev says. "In my head, there were two scenarios: Either the birth goes well, I'm well, and I'll be back in two weeks' time, or I'm in total baby mode and come back in six month's time. Based on that, I made a plan A and a plan B."

Luckily, everything went fine, and Louise took part in the first status meeting via Skype two weeks after giving birth.

"One month later, we met at my place. I planned my work before going on maternity leave so I always had my iPhone and my laptop with me. I can work from home; otherwise, I take my daughter Elna with me to the office. I don't work when she's awake, because I want to be with her and not regret anything later. My boyfriend is on partial paternity leave, and only works three days a week. When he's with Elna, I can work and hold meetings, so it works great.

"We've applied for daycare for when Elna is nine months, which is in July. But I'll have to see if she and I are ready, or otherwise I'll just continue taking her with me. I enjoy being with her, so I'll make it up as I go along.

"Jens only starts at 11am, and I'm counting on taking advantage of the flexibility that comes from being my own boss and start early. That way, I can pick her up early, and she gets long, cosy mornings with her father," Louise Ferslev says.

Since Anja Lytzen started Lirum Larum Leg 11 years ago, she's had two more children, and now she's the mother of four children, aged 2 to 14. "I guess it's typical me not wanting to compromise – neither with my business ambitions nor my family dreams. Of course it's demanding, but my children are also a big source of inspiration for me, and make sure I don't forget to play, go on adventures and laugh. All of these are important values, both for my business and for me."

The first maternity leave as a business owner was with Leonora, when the firm had been running for about two years. At the time, she already had Sofie-Emilie and Sebastian, who attended kindergarten. When her mother heard that Anja was pregnant again, her remark was: "You might just as well sell the firm." But that thought never struck Anja. If possible, she was even more determined to prove that it could be done.

Anja's mother was, at the time, employed during the maternity leave, and that was a great help. Anja had a short maternity leave, and after that carried Leonora in a sling to work and had a playpen at the office.

"It was tough as nails, because you can't plan a baby's circadian rhythm and when she sleeps. My husband has always worked a lot in Germany, and that was an advantage, because I could work with a good conscience when the children were asleep. I'd accumulate work if he was at home too much, and I had to sit and have some cosy time with him or watch TV with him. We've had an au pair since having Leonora, because mainly I'm very much alone with the children on weekdays. She helps with food, laundry and cleaning. At Christmas, when I'm most busy, she also makes sure the youngest are picked up early. Before that, I dropped the children off round 9-10am and picked them up around 4pm, and resumed my work when they fell asleep. The first years I sat up til 1, 2, 3am. At times, it was too hard, and I was on the threshold of getting stress. That's the reason I've talked a lot with a coach along the way, who taught me to delegate more, and said that I should go for runs, and go out every day for at least 20 minutes before starting work, to clear my head."

Anja had learned from her experiences and wanted to prepare better before having her fourth child, so there was more time to enjoy him. "I'm absolutely crazy about babies, and dreamt of enjoying maternity leave at home. So, a year before we got Sebastian, I hired a general manager and taught her the ropes, so I could take time off when he was born. The period up to the birth was tough, because we had to move the firm to new, larger premises one month before. It was both physically and mentally trying. I had two weeks' maternity leave, and then started coming in once a week, where I answered mails, followed up, and spoke to the employees, and then I slowly escalated with more days a week. After three months' maternity leave, one of my employees quit, and I got a text message from one of the other employees, who really didn't want to disturb me, but thought I should know that they were all on their way out," Anja recalls.

Unfortunately, the chemistry with the new leader wasn't good enough, and Anja was forced to fire her to keep her staff. Anja still had a couple of days at home, but mentally she was always at work. "It's hard not being able to park it."

Anja made some quick changes and reorganized, so three of her key employees were given added responsibility and the woman who had quit chose to stay. Instead of finding a new leader, one was put in charge of packaging, another in charge of the warehouse, and the third in charge of managing daily orders and operations. This was the right decision for the business and the employees, and Anja says: "It strengthened our bond, and we all pulled together with a common feeling of wanting to show that we can succeed. What seemed hopeless before, became good and positive within a couple of weeks, when the changes had been implemented."

Luckily, the workload has lessened with time, and the balance is easier, as earnings and the children both grew and Anja hired more staff.

"My personal goal has been to breathe easier in December, and in 2016, I managed to be at home and eat dinner with them the whole month. It's a milestone I'm well pleased with. I rarely work evenings anymore, and most of the time I have regular 9 to 4 working days. Now it's nice, because the big ones can be a part of it in a different way. The children put stickers on, help out and come along when parcels are delivered at the post office. Sebastian helped out this year, and Sofie-Emilie will be going to camp in 7th grade, so she and her classmates will be coming to work here to earn money for the trip."

Everyday Life Has to Work

Birgitte Feldborg is the mother of five, her husband works a lot, and she lives in the countryside where public transport is not as frequent so she always drives the children. She has organized herself in such a way that she has a home office, where she works most of the time, and an office in town, that she uses for meetings.

Birgitte's working time is structured, so she's sure to get through the most important things.

"I work from about 8am to 4pm. Every Friday, I make a plan for the coming week, with meetings and appointments, as well as the three most important tasks I have to do every day. Now the children are bigger, but I'm always at home when they come back from school. It's great. They always pop in the office and chat about the day's events. Then I usually continue working while they relax a bit.

"From 4-5pm we do homework together and there are buns and tea. They manage quite well on their own, but it really helps them to stay motivated having me there. After that, I make dinner and read professional books for myself. We eat around 6.30-7.30pm, as my husband, Ole, comes home around then. Then I put the youngest to bed.

In the evenings, I spend a lot of my time on the volunteer work that I do because I want to do something social and help those less fortunate than us," Birgitte says.

"One of the reasons why I can do all this," she adds, " is that we have an au pair who takes care of all the housework, so I don't have to think of that. Weekends are dedicated to close family, my house and my garden. In particular, my mother, who's widowed, often stops by and has a nice time with us. It's important for me that also she feels good."

Birgitte has experienced most changes in terms of friends.

"When it comes to friends, I've paid a high price. We've grown more and more apart, and don't have that much in common. The mental part in particular separates us, because I believe one has to assume responsibility, and the world is not to blame if one's working life isn't what one wishes. Today, I only have new friends left, and they are all self-employed."

Having self-employed friends also has its advantages. "Being a mother is a full-time job, so working time is 'my' time. There has to be room to catch your breath, so here I also include appointments at the hairdresser's and lunch with my self-employed friends. It's important that my life should function as a whole, instead of in just one area. There has to be room for family, work and me."

Louise Ertman Baunsgaard is a good example of how you can have children while expanding your business. They had their first daughter, Amalie, when Louise was opening her fourth restaurant and a year and a half later, after Olivia was born. Louise only had two weeks' maternity leave and then took her babies to work.

"First year with two small kids is hard, but you forget fast," Louise explains. "My mother does the bookkeeping at Letz Sushi, and she was always there to help me with the children. My husband travels a lot in his job, so I have always spent a lot of time with our children, but quickly found a nanny to help a couple of hours a day. That was my free time to work."

Louise is extremely efficient and focused when she works and gets a lot done in little time. "When the girls were small, I only worked about 25 hours a week and I've rarely worked more than 40 hours since Letz Sushi was established," she confirms. "When you own a business, work becomes your identity and life, so it is important to know when to say stop and remember to prioritize your personal life and family. Creating a business is a journey; you should enjoy the freedom of being your own boss instead of working yourself to death for four years to make a quick sell."

Motherhood and business worked out so well for Louise that she felt like having more children, and she had her third child, William, when her daughters were four and five.

Partner or Family Support

Before you embark upon the self-employed entrepreneur's journey, it's important that you have a conversation with your husband, partner or boyfriend to match expectations – both in relation to the home front and your business.

- Who takes care of house chores?
- Should food be homemade or are sandwiches good enough when you're busy?
- How many after-school activities should the children have each and are you going to attend all their matches or shows?
- Should you bake for events or will store-bought cakes do?
- How often should you see family and friends?
- Should you, yourselves have activities in your spare time?
- Who stays at home with the children when they're sick?
- Whose career or work is more important?

And so on.

Often, it's the practical things that make everything collapse. It's important to work as a team and find the solutions together, so one person isn't left carrying the can.

It's not unusual that the man's career is more important because he earns more money, especially when the self-employed entrepreneur woman is in the starting phase of her business. Your bills have to be paid, of course, but it can be really hard to succeed if you need to be an attentive mother, do all the house chores and run your business. A solution to the problem is often getting help on the home front with the cleaning, cutting down on the expectations of homemade baked goods and freshly ironed clothes, as well as organizing carpools with other parents, and leaning on grandparents or other close relatives.

Birgitte Othel has a husband who travels a lot, and he can be gone for up to two weeks at a time.

"I made a very tight schedule when the children were small. My husband, Erik, travelled a lot, so I had to structure my time. I had a cosy morning and dropped off the youngest at 9.30am. I worked on my computer from 10am to 4pm, and then I picked up the children. We had some family time, I served them dinner and then put them to bed. When Erik was home, we ate dinner together at 8pm and enjoyed time together," Birgitte Othel says.

"The time from 4pm to 8pm has always been dedicated to my children. It was important for me to be there when they came home. I could always work in the evening, or on the weekend, if they were out. For many years, they didn't know I was self-employed, and they thought Mum just sat at home drawing.

"When Erik is away, I get help from his parents with the children. You need some kind of help in the home, from family or close friends, if everyday life is to function. One thing I can recommend to others who have husbands who are often away, is to communicate. I always briefed Erik over the phone the day before he came home. So, he was up to date on everything and could talk with the children about what had just happened in their lives. During the course of the week, I wrote down everything, from birthdays to lost teeth, so I didn't forget to tell him about anything. Erik recorded our conversation and listened to it again on the plane on his way home. It helped him to stay up to date – and it was really good for the marriage, because I didn't feel that I was left with all of the work," Birgitte says.

Besides having a look at your everyday life, you and your partner should also match expectations in terms of the financial aspects. As a self-employed entrepreneur, your financial situation can go up and down, which in itself is demanding and nerve-wracking. You don't need your family pressuring you or not being understanding towards your situation. Make it quite clear what you're going to earn. How much do you two want to invest in the business? And how you are going to do it. For example, are you going to cut down on your joint consumption for a while, so there's more leeway in the budget for your business?

Even if the business is your dream, you share a common life that must work, and you have a joint responsibility to find a solution. All the women I interviewed had moral support from their husbands. But that doesn't necessarily mean that their husbands were able to help them any more than before they started their business, or that they were there a lot, because as you can read, many of the men were focused on their own careers. But communicating and being on the same page helps everyone know what the plan is and not have one's partner complaining about the money or trying to stop you from living out your dream.

Be Efficient

To make the most of your time, it's important you know where you're heading. In this case, your vision is your goal, and your strategy plan is the road you should stick to in order to get there quickly and safely.

Being self-employed you wear many hats, and there are rarely enough hours in the day. When you're also a mother, and want to spend time with your children, even more is asked of you, and you will need to prioritize your time and optimize your resources if you want to do it all without breaking down. Of course, there's always the possibility of there being periods with illness and the like, which are extra trying, but otherwise your everyday life should work and you should also be able to breathe.

To date, I've held several workshops on how to become more efficient in everyday life. Some people may start sweating at the prospect of being more efficient as they associate that with working faster and more, which can be rather stressful. My starting point when working with efficiency is that I must be more productive and create better results when I'm working, so I can take time off and be with my family with a clear conscience, without having to think of everything I have to do.

We recently moved. It's taken time. There was lots to do with packing, moving, taking care of administration and so on, especially because we had three months from the time we sold our flat until we could move into the new house, during which time we had to live in a third place. Also, we couldn't get day care for the twins, so they had to change kindergarten three times in four months. Luckily, I successfully structured my work, without that affecting my earnings – so I hardly needed to do anything for work during most of this time. For me, being efficient is optimizing my resources. In this step, I want to give you tools and shortcuts to being efficient when you're working, so you can make time to be with those who mean the most to you.

Focus

Being self-employed, we easily get lots of ideas, and we want to act upon all of them. The challenge is that everyone can get ideas, but only a few can carry them out. That's also the reason why many investors and Business Angels hold back on putting money into a business or a project until they've seen that those behind it can narrow down and work with their idea.

Here it's important you're aware that your brain often plays tricks on you and tries to lead you astray when you identify an idea that means something to you and is uncertain. I usually call them procrastination acts in disguise, because they're so well hidden you don't notice them if you're not paying attention to them. Procrastination often appears under the disguise of good ideas that seem so solid that you can convince yourself and others that they're important to bring to fruition here and now.

A classic example is when we feel there's just one thing we have to learn first before we can do what really matters. I meet highly educated women, who've already taken oodles of courses and feel they need one more. While it's good to educate yourself and learn something new, that shouldn't hinder your success. One of my clients holds lectures where she talks about how she and her husband followed their dream and sailed around the world with their children. She wanted to hold more lectures to earn more money, as she was finding it hard make ends meet. She asked me if it was a good idea to study coaching. If she wanted to be a coach it'd be the obvious choice, but to get more clients it'd be more relevant to learn about sales and marketing, or pay to get help preparing her sales process. It happens to us all; we all get misleading ideas, so it's important to consider if the idea will help you reach your goal, or if it's just a tempting opportunity to do something that doesn't take you out of your comfort zone.

When taking a course, the hardest thing is not the course itself; it's using what you've learned afterwards on a daily basis. The purchase of a new course, especially if it's online, can easily become a quick fix that makes you believe you have found the solution, but if you don't act upon what you've learned, it's just a waste of precious time and money.

It can be incredibly tempting to try many things at the same time, and I'm sure you can provide oodles of good reasons to do so. At times like this, it's important to concretize and return to your original goal. Why did you start your own business? What kind of life do you want to have? How much time do you want to spend with your family? How much do you want/must you earn?

If you're doing too many things, everything will take longer, you'll have more work to do and you will be earning less money. For many people, having more to do also puts them under unnecessary pressure, and they end up feeling insecure because they don't get results. The question is if you're willing to pay the price and accept the consequences of having too many balls in the air, or if you instead choose to focus.

Stick to one target group, one product or one idea, and focus. Work with it until you succeed; otherwise, although you will be doing a lot in many areas, in the end you will get nowhere. Start with the idea that gives you the most energy, and gather other ideas in a folder or a document so you can refer to them later, or buy a domain name, so you needn't worry about other people snatching it.

Go all in for what you're doing; concentrate on the tasks that have to be done, then the results will come. A common problem with many self-employed entrepreneurs is that they grind to a halt or give up, they grow impatient for results, start doubting what they're doing. Whereas successful business owners proactively focus on the key things, without expecting immediate results, and thus have the capacity to work faster towards their goal.

Systems, Habits, Automation

Self-discipline is hard and often demands effort. Luckily, there's a lot you can do to support yourself in making the right decisions and staying on track.

Systems and habits can help to make the most of your time and get more done. We often waste a lot of time thinking about things instead of acting. We think about whether it feels good, if we want to do something or how things will go, instead of actually doing what we should be doing. Systematize your work and create good habits you can lean on and use to get a lot more done. Direct your thoughts to where they make a difference. In this way, you will ensure that the most important things get done first, and that you don't get distracted.

Sales and marketing, online or direct, is a task we all have to do. You have to do it every week so you can continually create new contacts that may turn into new clients. If you set a fixed time for it in your calendar, you'll ensure a flow in your earnings. Many self-employed entrepreneurs who do their own bookkeeping may find it to be a boring and laborious task. But it's important to do it on an ongoing basis, so it doesn't pile up and become chaotic.

A good habit is starting every day doing the most important things first, before checking emails or going on the internet. Studies show that you become 30% more efficient if you wait and start working on your emails and internet-related activity until around 10am. Emails often seem important, and one may be inclined to answer them at once, but unless you're expecting a very important answer from a client, hold off handling them until you've gone through what you'd set yourself to do. The thing is, there are only a limited number of decisions you can make a day before you get tired and start to make bad decisions. The phenomenon is called decision fatigue. That's why you must use your resources and your mental surplus for what's important in the morning, before allowing yourself to be disturbed by other people's queries or information on the net. For the same reason, it can be a good idea to sleep on a decision if you're tired. Eliminating daily decisions can really help this; for instance, if you're the one who does the cooking and the shopping, it may be a good idea to make a meal plan or have food delivered, so you don't have to make decisions about that every day. If you want to be really hard-core and focused, like Steve Jobs and some other successful business people, you can have many sets of the same clothes and not waste time deciding what to wear every day. Alternatively, you can minimize your wardrobe or get help from a stylist if this isn't your passion.

A great time saver is using the phone when you want to get a hold of someone about something important. It's an easy and safe habit sending an email or a text message, but at the same time, it puts you on hold and leaves it to the recipient to reply in their own time. We've become so accustomed to online tools that many feel it's unpleasant to call others, especially if we don't know them that well. It may seem trivial, but I see it all the time with self-employed entrepreneurs who wait and wait and get nowhere, instead of grabbing the phone and getting an answer. Of course, it's because we're afraid of disturbing people, or don't want to get a no. But no matter the answer, it's better to find out earlier. Also, it's actually easier to answer no or reject someone by email. But, when you speak to someone, they're required to listen to what you're saying, plus the dialogue often provides the possibility to get some answers and dispel misunderstandings one wouldn't have discovered in an email.

Studies show that when influencing others, 7% is what we say, 38% is our voice, and 55% is our body language. So ideally physical meetings get better results, but if you can't meet in person, the phone is better than email.

In general, I prioritize face-to-face meetings over emails or phone calls when it's time to close a deal with a large company. In a face-to-face, I have the opportunity to go through the deal, handle possible objections and get the client's ongoing approval. This benefits me and the other party in that we can more efficiently get to a price that works for both of us and sign the deal there and then. If you don't meet with your client, you risk something or someone external disturbing and perhaps even spoiling the development of the deal without you being able to do anything about it.

Apart from your habits and systems, you can also automate some of your daily tasks. As mentioned before, I use an online payment system so I don't have to send out invoices, and I've automated part of my newsletter so that I'm sure that everyone who signs up gets the knowledge and an introduction to my firm the way I want it.

For example, several of my clients who sell physical products use a warehouse and a post order firm to deal with orders, so that they don't have to pack and send out goods themselves. A practice that worked for me when I was in recruitment was having a template for all kinds of emails and job adverts that my assistant worked with. Being more automated may require an investment of some kind in a product that enables automation of a part of your business, but the investment should save you so much time and you should recoup it somewhere else.

That leads me to the next aspect you can work on, namely investing and getting help.

Invest and Get Help

Many business owners are afraid of spending money. Of course, it's because you don't have that much in the beginning, but it's really hard saving your way to success. Where you can, you should invest. I say 'invest' on purpose, and try not to 'spend money', because you should get a return on your investment. There are many tasks you have to take into account; accountancy, sales, marketing, product development, customer service, etc. Here it's important that you don't get lost in tasks you're not very good at, and waste your time, but rather that you spend most of your time doing what you're good at.

A classic example is your homepage. Most people want to save money in the beginning and make their own homepage. It seems like an appealing solution, as there are many free templates and systems available. But if you're not technically gifted, it can easily turn into a huge time-waster. What often happens is that you spend a long time making a page that in the end isn't optimal. The time you spend on this is time you should be doing much more important things, namely getting clients, which allows you to be able to live off what you do. Your time and your energy are better spent getting visitors to your home-page or going out and being visible in other places where your clients are.

Anja Lytzen's choice of investing right away in a graphic designer, and getting help to make the Lirum Larum Leg's homepage, is a good example of knowing your weaknesses and getting help with what you can't do properly your-self. Because her homepage was good when she launched, many clients came at once and because they were satisfied, they then recommended it to others.

When you invest, you must be aware of what you want to get out of the investment, and how big it should be. A homepage can cost from £500 to over £10,000 to make, so you ought to know what your needs are and how much time that frees up for you to do other things. Not all busi-nesses need an expensive homepage; just look at Albi's Kaffebar that only uses Facebook.

It's also important that you don't go from one extreme to another and think that your investment can solve all your problems. If we take the example of the homepage, you pay to get a homepage, but that doesn't get you cli-ents. If being short on clients is your problem, you must have either a homepage and keyword search engine opti-mization, or a homepage and ads, or another solution that sends people to your homepage. Also, the content of your homepage has to be good enough for people to buy something, contact you or sign up for your newsletter. For example, Anja spent her time getting people's email addresses and doing PR, so she was able to get a lot of vis-itors to the Lirum Larum Leg homepage.

Investments are rarely miracles, but they can save you time and yield some results. One might think or hope that an investment can give you the clients you lack. It's still your responsibility to make things work.

Some self-employed entrepreneurs wrongly believe that a single strategy session can turn their situation around. The session can give them a plan and a lot of important knowledge, but they still have to implement the plan and create results.

Analyse and Optimize

At times it is helpful to look at what you've done and analyse the results. By analysing your work, you'll get an idea of what works, what can be improved and what you really should stop doing. The most important is that your earnings are bigger than your investment.

One of my clients sells several different products and has a good turnover, but she doesn't really earn that much. By analysing her figures, we found that one of the products wasn't selling very well. When we removed this product from stock and added different products, her earnings increased visibly in the course of a couple of weeks and that turned it into a healthy business.

Even if you think that you can only make minor adjustments that will not make that big a difference, it's important to see the big picture. Try accumulating things over a longer period of time, and you'll see a bigger difference even with small changes. For example, let's say that by making a tiny change you can save or earn £5 more a day. In a year, that totals £1,825.

It's not only in relation to money that you should analyse and optimize, but also what you spend your time on, what results that generates and if you can do it better. One hour a day is 365 hours a year, equivalent to about nine weeks' full-time work.

When you optimize, it's sometimes about searching for easier solutions. A cheap and easy solution is not necessarily worse than one that's expensive and complicated. Anna Bogdanova can attest to that.

"You can't delegate everything from the start. I tried that, and I spent far too much money on unnecessary things such as design and homepage. It's better to take it one day at a time and not force it. It mustn't be too hard. If so, you have to find an easier way or solution. You needn't crawl down the chimney when the door's open. It's better to be open to easier solutions when you're in the midst of it.

"In the beginning, I was my own bottleneck for a number of years. Every time we grew, there was me, the bottleneck, but there was a way past it. You mustn't give up. Just because something doesn't work, you're not a failure," Anna says. "I challenge people who want to have everything on Excel spreadsheets. I think in a chaotic way, and I can encompass the chaos people can't control. Maybe they're in control on the surface, but there are always areas that are a mess. That's why I'm not stringent. I do what's best for the clients, or my child, in the given situation."

Exercise: Get an Overview of Your Tasks

At the end of Step 1, I asked you to make an overview of your work tasks and to divide them into strengths, weaknesses and fears. Now it's time to look at them and find out what you'll do about them.

- Look at the overview and add up how much time you spend on the different tasks, either per week or per month.
- Look at the results each task yields, and if any of them cost money. Typically, 20% of your work should lead to 80% of your results. For example, you may be spending time and money working on 'useless' details for your homepage.
- List the tasks that you can do but take a long time to complete and don't create results, delegate these tasks and use this time to earn money. Maybe you can even drop some of them entirely?

- Think of the tasks that you are not needed for or are not good, and decide which can be given to others to take care of. It can be bookkeeping, updating the homepage, packing and sending goods, proofreading, getting someone to be in your shop when you're out purchasing new goods and so on.
- The important work tasks, where you feel your fear stops you, you can seek to discuss in your network to your advantage, or you can get a coach or a mentor who can help you move on with the process.

Delegate and Use Others as Sounding Boards

Getting outside help needn't be as expensive as you might fear. Nowadays, there are many opportunities to get a virtual assistant; you can get a student or a jobseeker doing an internship or pay a freelancer. That way, you don't need a full-time employee, and you can adjust the amount of help up or down so it fits your business needs. What is key is that you can streamline some of your work routines by making use of the possibilities available and free up time to work on the areas that are important.

Besides getting help with practical tasks, sometimes you need to use others as sounding boards and get help from people who've come further than you with their business. There's no reason to spend your energy reinventing the wheel every time you do something new. Here, your network and your mentors can be of great help. We often think we're alone with our challenges, but by talking to other self-employed people, you'll realize that's it's the same for everybody. The advantage is that we've reached different places with our businesses, have different skills, and can share our knowledge and lift one another up.

In my networking meetings and workshops, participants breathe a sigh of relief and laughter breaks out when I discuss the challenges we have all come across. By sharing such challenges, you can help someone who hasn't come as far as you, and receive valuable feedback and advice. The internet and the media can give a warped image of how it is to run a business and how others are doing, so it's always good to get a reality check among your peers.

An experience that's given me a lot of support was when I was on a four-day seminar in California to learn about High Performance. There were participants from all over the world; some had held TED talks, others had written bestsellers or earned many millions. It was lovely to see that they were perfectly normal people – they had no special powers, but they had worked in a goal-oriented way to turn their dreams into reality. It made me believe that I would succeed with my business if I only kept at it and didn't give up. Like everybody else, I also face challenges and this experience helped remind me to keep going forward.

Having a mentor can be beneficial, and if you choose the right mentor, they can save you from the many distractions and detours so that you get further, faster. By the right one, I mean that you should find a person who has experience and has created results within the area you need help. Someone who's been down the same road as you. I tried working with an American mentor who was really good at working with the inner hindrances, such as fear and inhibiting convictions, and motivating. But unfortunately she couldn't help me strategically, as her approach was too American for the Danish market. It was a tough lesson to learn. So, before choosing one or more mentors, consider what results they should help you achieve. Is it to motivate you, make you good at a particular skill, like holding speeches or writing books, or should they help your business enter a new market and get more clients?

All in all, it's a smart idea to surround yourself with people who understand what it means to own a business and who understand your challenges, priorities and dreams. Very few employees will be able to put themselves in your position, and they'll often present you with uncomprehending and unnecessary concerns. They probably mean well, but it doesn't always feel supportive. It can be quite draining always having to answer their worries. There are topics that I only discuss with my entrepreneur friends, and I'd never dream of discussing them with my family or old friends.

I have since discovered that's it's quite liberating not discussing my business with everyone. Often, my head is quite full of my business, and it feels like a breath of fresh air seeing a friend, where we laugh and speak about of other things. The danger of being so personally engaged in your work is that it can take up too much space, and you can lose your sense of perspective, so what happens in your business might seem larger and more important than it perhaps really is.

Network – and on Daring to Ask for Help

You can't know everything. A key to success is daring to ask for help and finding the people who have the skills you need.

Louise Ferslev from MyMonii has purposefully held many meetings and networked with important contacts who have been able to lift her business. She looked for an experienced Chief Technology Officer (CTO) who could take charge of the company's technological infrastructure.

"I met some people at an event in 2015 who were interested in my story and remembered me from some of the meetings I held early on when I had started my business. They wanted to help MyMonii, and I asked them to help me find a good CTO. They pointed to Alex, whom I'd met a couple of times. The chemistry was there from the very start, and now he's at the company three days a week, as he also owns his own firm on the side," Louise says.

Besides finding a CTO, Louise has also used the many meetings and network activities to create a good advisory board.

"When I meet people at work-related events that I have good chemistry with, I always invite them for coffee afterwards and ask for their help. Everyone says yes when asked politely. One must not underestimate how good people are at helping one another. I call them when I have questions that relate to their skills, and in the past, I've gathered them for the presentation of a case. I've learned so much from them."

Hire and Delegate

When you have a lot to do, there comes a time when you have to decide if you should get help from others to solve some of your tasks, either by outsourcing or by hiring an employee. There are advantages and disadvantages to both solutions, and what's best for you depends to a great extent on what you want to do with your business and your everyday life. I myself have tried both. In Paris, we quickly hired assistants, and for me the help was incredibly valuable. Sarah was great at screening applications, doing phone interviews and calling people in for interviews. She was also good at finding specialists and inviting the right candidate for an interview. This made it possible for me to concentrate on the interviews, test the applicants and hold meetings with clients. Sarah was often also present in meetings with clients and interviews, and she wrote reports, so I needn't worry about writing correct French, either. With her by my side, I could solve twice as many tasks at a time.

The disadvantage, seen through my eyes, of having employees, is that one has to be very present. It requires leadership to motivate your employees, and despite the fact that they can manage a lot of freedom responsibly, it's always your responsibility to make sure that things run smoothly. Therefore, in Mors Business I've also chosen to outsource some tasks to others, and every now and again cooperate with other business owners on different projects. It's nice, and at the same time I get more business out of it. At the moment, my hands are full, being the mother of four, and I don't want to be anybody's boss, but that might change when the children get older.

Birgitte Feldborg says she also tested the waters, until she reached the conclusion that she fares best as solo self-employed. "I've had three different employees, and I can't be bothered to have that responsibility. It's a big burden. I have to be present at all times, and get them working, and I have to find enough work for them all the time, even though one of the requirements of the job was being able to take the initiative and contribute to get new tasks. I'd rather hire a freelancer and pay that bill. Over time, the freelancers I've cooperated with have almost become like colleagues."

Louise Ertman Baunsgaard's strategy was, from the start, to hire qualified help. She wasn't a sushi cook and never planned to become one, either. She knew her strengths were in marketing and developing the concept and that she wanted to open more than one restaurant. Having employees is part of her success, but also a big responsibility.

"When you want to run a restaurant, having employees is part of the game, and I never considered it otherwise. However, many women start their own business to gain more freedom and, in that respect, employees are a huge responsibility that takes up a lot of your time. Should I start over again, I might chose a business model where I could hire external help without employing anybody," Louise reckons.

Courage and
Determination

Whatever the situation, you have to take responsibility. Nobody will come and feel sorry for you and build your business for you. You might be having bad luck in your life right now, but it's your responsibility to move forward and create the life you want to have.

Luckily, it isn't always about having many resources to build a business you can live off. It's about having courage and determination. A good example of being resourceful is Pia Nissen Tylak. With two businesses, she's shown in two very different ways that having no money, or even being in debt, is no impediment to success. The first time was when she bought the creative business Schillerhuset, with more than 100 workers. At the time, she'd never owned a business before, but circumstances would have it that she chose to take the plunge, because she was afraid the employees would lose their jobs if the business was purchased by a big advertising agency. Pia herself had started at Schillerhuset four years before. She didn't have the relevant education and was met with prejudice from the other shareholders due to her background as a model. Luckily, Leif Schiller knew her privately, and could see the potential.

"I immediately jumped into new markets, where they weren't established yet, and quickly got many new clients. Shortly after, I was hired full-time as studio manager and saleswoman and the other shareholders slowly came to recognize my skills," says Pia, who quickly advanced in the firm. "People mean a lot to me, so people automatically came to me when they were feeling down, or needed help. I was chosen as employee representative on the board of directors, and after that I became the HR manager."

Pia talks about the time when the business was to add a new director: "I took part in the talks, together with the headhunter firm and the board of directors. They were looking for a man with an MBA in economics, but in my eyes what the firm needed was more cooperation across the board, and new approaches that would focus on people. In a break between two talks, I asked if they shouldn't save a lot of money and take me instead," Pia says. The chief financial officer (CFO) answered that they wanted to find "the right gentleman." They did find a competent man for the job, but it turned out that he had received a better offer and didn't want the job after all. The board of directors held an emergency meeting, where they decided to temporarily appoint Pia, until they found a new *gentleman* for the job.

It was now that Pia had to prove she was the right one for the job. "I wanted to show the board that a woman could definitely do the job, and despite being pregnant, I beavered away to bring people together, create networks and results, and three months later, I was offered the position."

There was to be a generational change, and Leif Schiller was offered an eight-figure amount by an advertising agency. Pia was worried about the bid, as she feared the present workers would be fired in favour of those already working for the advertising agency. Pia was driven by passion and love for people, and she wanted to take over the business herself to protect their jobs. This was the starting point for her desire to become self-employed, and she asked the bank how much she could borrow to buy the business. She could only borrow a small fraction of the amount the advertising agency had bid but even so, she went to Leif Schiller with her bid, and offered to continue the business in his spirit, because it was about more than just money. Leif accepted, and thus Pia became a self-employed director at the age of 30.

Many would say that Pia was lucky to be able to buy the business so cheaply, but together with the responsibility for 100 creative people, there also came millions in debt she had to see to. But Pia wasn't worried. She worked in a goal-oriented manner towards creating a workplace with passion, love and no sharp elbows, where she supported the workers to be successful. And it worked.

"Some people think I got Schillerhuset cheap, but I took over six million in debt! My accountant said I shouldn't. But I had enough self-confidence, and I was sure I'd find solutions. Opportunities appear when you're in the flow. With Schillerhuset, I took a photography house and turned it into a community for multi-creative people. I sold off one department. I got an investor and a partner, and I turned the situation around," Pia says.

After six years at Schillerhuset, many things happened in Pia's life that made her downscale and leave the company, in order to start afresh with her two daughters in the south of Jutland, where she'd found love.

Pia knew she didn't want to be an employee, but rather she wanted to start a new self-owned business. She had no starting capital or network where she was moving to, but she believed in her dreams.

"I started by writing and telling the mayor about my passion and my desire to create something unique in the municipality that would keep the young, creative talents from leaving. The mayor agreed to meet with me and when we did, I presented a six-month plan for the project. The mayor agreed to support me by offering to put a building at my disposal. I wanted to continue on the same track as at Schillerhuset and create a unique community for creative people. That was the beginning of The Creative House that still exists. Here I helped the creative succeed by working on their personal development."

Personal development was something that had interested Pia for many years, so at the same time as she started The Creative House, she also started another business:

Spirit Academy. Here the focus was solely on personal development, and Pia dreamt of living off her own experiences and her passion, and used what she had learned from the coaching and self-development courses. When she'd got The Creative House up and running, she let go of the project to dedicate herself to Spirit Academy.

Pia's story shows that you can get far with the right vision and the courage to say out loud what you want. Pia got a yes for both, because she had the guts to go after what she wanted and found win-win solutions for both parties. By telling Leif Schiller and the mayor of the Aabenraa municipality what they could get out of helping her, and how her ideas would benefit them, she got their approval.

Go Outside Your Comfort Zone

Coming across tasks that are on the edge or outside of our comfort zone can trigger a wave of procrastination and unleash many thoughts that grow bigger if one doesn't stop them. It can be a real time stealer, because you spend time on all kinds of things, or you freeze up. When certain people are described as brave, it's often because they act even if they're scared, or take a risk and expose themselves to a potential failure. As mentioned in the first step, courage can be trained, and the more you do it, the easier it gets.

Anja from Lirum Larum Leg didn't like doing interviews at all in the beginning, and she found public speaking exceedingly unpleasant.

"In connection with my nomination to the yearly One of a Kind award in 2017, I'm going to pitch before 800 people. I feel really nauseous, get palpitations and my stomach aches. I use far too many mental resources preparing myself, and I refused to in the past, but I still think it'd be silly not to pitch now that I'm nominated and can win a nice award," Anja told me.

Anja did it last week all the same, with butterflies in her stomach – and with great support from her employees.

In the aftermath, she concluded that, "We got no award this evening, but never mind; I'm still surrounded by the world's best colleagues, and we will continue running the business with our hearts. Even though no award came out of this, I still felt as though I won by standing on the stage and pitching."

You do not need to challenge yourself all the time, but the easiest way to push yourself is to take one step at a time.

Take Your Needs Seriously

Many (men in particular) erroneously believe that when my work focuses on helping mothers, it's because they're incompetent or not serious enough as business people. That's until I explain that self-employed mothers are extra tough because besides running a business, they must also have the surplus energy to be a present and good mother. Nature dictates that we should be the ones to bear children, give birth and nurse. Even though we're getting closer to equality, and many men are more actively involved in family life, it's still the mother who, in particular during the first years, spends more time with the children. The large amounts of hormones in the body send us on an emotional roller coaster ride, and lack of sleep enhances that.

Being a mother can be trying. Having your own business can be trying. But both require you to look after yourself if you want to do both at the same time. In order to be able to continue giving to your children and to your business, you must be good to yourself and remember to recharge your energy. Can you allow yourself to do so as self-employed? Yes, because otherwise you'll run yourself down.

To make up for that, I don't watch TV in the evening, but I work if I'm not too tired.

To keep having the necessary extra energy to develop your business and be there for your family, it's important to take good care of yourself and really prioritize your sleep, your nutrition and your physical activity on a daily basis. It can be tempting to work late nights, or relax in front of the TV or Facebook or to have a glass of red wine with your friends and have a good time. But if it happens too often, it'll take its toll on your energy and your mood. You won't work so well the day after, and you're less patient and present towards those closest to you. You decide, but consider what means most to you. What do you want in the long run? What do you most want to rejoice about when you look back on your life?

Our bodies are geared to go for immediate, quick gratification, so it takes willpower to make healthy, mature choices, but it's the sum total of your daily actions that yields results. It doesn't mean you can't have fun, but it must be enjoyed in limited portions, if it's not to affect your health.

Also, it's important to eat healthy and take part in physical activity and get some fresh air. Exercise is revitalising and improves your mood; it also helps you think in a goal-oriented way when faced with challenges. You get other perspectives when you're outdoors, compared with when you are sat staring at a computer screen. Choose an activity you think is fun and that is easy to do, so you aren't tempted to skip it.

If you're serious about your business and your family, you must also take your own health seriously. As a parent, you often give high priority to the physical activity and social relations of your children, but it is important to also invest in yourself. I have a good friend, who dreamed of 24 hours at a luscious hotel with massage, spa and a three-course menu, while her husband looked after the children. I myself have invested in everything from short courses that have boosted my motivation, given me inspiration and new knowledge for my business, to a personal trainer, who got me training again and ensured I got physical strength and energy to get through a lot.

There's really a lot of self-development connected with being self-employed, and you must develop at the same pace as your business, and stock up on knowledge and well-being if you're to keep up with, and grow, your business.

A Big
Wake-up Call

Pia Nissen Tylak has been self-employed now for nearly 20 years and has herself experienced how a situation can turn bad if your heart and mind aren't in it. Pia took a Higher Preparatory Examination and worked a number of years as a model before she became a business owner by taking over Schillerhuset. She was firmly determined to shatter all prejudice and show that as the young mother of small children she could power through, turn the business around and create profits. Pia says she had a little daughter and had her second child while she was self-employed: "I worked from home during the first maternity leave; the second time, I was back full-time a mere five days after giving birth, and my newborn daughter came with me to all meetings. All in all, I worked a lot while the children were young. Back then, I thought it was ok to work 70 hours a week, though I always made sure to pick up my girls, and instead work late into the evening, while they were asleep."

In hindsight, Pia can tell there were many signs that she was too busy.

"For example, when Amanda was little, I was quite forgetful. I brought her to work with me, so there were some simple practical issues with getting the pram out of the car, remembering the bag, turning on the alarm, and so on. One day, when I was leaving for home, and put the car in reverse in the parking lot, I heard a thump. I had run over something, but I couldn't see what it was at first. It turned out that I'd put my computer in a tote bag, and set it against the back wheel and forgotten all about it."

Pia managed to get rid of Schillerhuset's debt and create an efficient business. She worked a lot and did everything she could for her workers to thrive and blossom, both personally and professionally. At the same time, Pia wanted to prove her worth and fight the prejudice surrounding her. Adding to that, a lot happened in her personal life that affected her. Her father committed suicide, and Leif Schiller, who she describes as her life's mentor, passed away. In the process, she forgot herself and her needs, and gradually became more and more stressed. Pia felt these stresses took their toll on her health.

"I had a heart attack due to stress that nearly cost me my life, because I lost my sight driving on a motorway. Miraculously, I managed to get off the road without hurting anyone. I had an intense near-death experience, and the experience was a great shock. The only thing I thought about was seeing my girls, and holding them again, before I was taken to hospital."

"It was my life's greatest wake-up call. I'd neglected myself for too long. Luckily, I regained my sight, and nothing serious happened, but I chose to reprioritize my life, and give it a 180-degree turn. I left the girls' father and made a plan to downscale and leave Schillerhuset. Love for me and my girls would be the top priority from now on. I moved to southern Jutland, where I started afresh, both personally and work wise," Pia Nissen Tylak says.

Pia wanted to earn money with The Creative House, while the Spirit Academy got started. Both businesses started off well, because Pia was true to her heart, followed her intuition, and used her broad experience from before to create something better.

"I'd travelled the world, and been taught by several 'transformative leaders', among others Louise Hay, Wayne Dyer, Tony Robbins, Brian Mayne and Janet Atwood, and a number of them are still my friends today. I wanted to use my coaching studies and experience to create a course that had what other courses lacked. I created the Executive Spirit Coach course that combines knowledge about communication, research, biology and spirituality.

"It took about six months to fill the first group for my course. I only used Facebook and sent emails to my contacts. I shared my own story, which others have been able to relate to and see themselves in. I have only had my homepage for the last three to four years."

It's paradoxical that Pia nowadays works less and earns more than she did as the director and owner of a large company.

"I've been alone with my girls the last three years, but I have more time now than I did before because I'm better at following my heart and I don't waste time on unnecessary battles. You avoid a lot of adversity when you follow your heart. The road gets shorter, because you know you're doing the right thing. The more I'm in my heart, and the more I have returned to my original essence, the more money I've earned, and the more time I've had for my children. I want to be there for my children. They are my everything.

"Freedom is also important to me. The freedom to be with those I love when I want, to do what I want, and have financial and emotional freedom," Pia says.

Pia is working on a new study, Intuitive Master, where she will help others bring out their clarity, so they can see all the opportunities that lie at their feet.

"You have to live by your values to succeed. You mustn't copy what others do. What's a good business for them isn't necessarily for you. You must work from the heart and create your own concept," she concludes.

Remember to Say No

You must also take yourself seriously when you're facing clients who aren't fair. The motto about the client always being right doesn't hold true. Your self-respect and professional pride are important, and you must not compromise just because some clients are difficult or narrow-minded.

Graphic designer Birgitte Othel has been self-employed for almost 25 years. She has had her fair share of difficult clients, and through that, she learned to draw a line of self-respect for herself. "In many areas, it's important to educate the clients and say no. For example, when I develop a logo for small business owners. It's hard, because the logo means so much to them, and they so want to have both recognition, a long story and nice graphics in the design, but at the same time they are conscious that it doesn't cost a lot. There's a lot of psychology in customer consulting, and I've included the many changes in my price, as I'd waste too much time otherwise on the clients' changing opinions. I love the process and when the clients are happy and satisfied because the final result reflects their business," Birgitte says.

Your clients can have many unrealistic demands. So, it's important to remember it's your business, and hang on to your opinion. But, many people have a misguided perception of a self-employed entrepreneur's time and work.

"They can ask: 'Can't you do this – that won't cost anything, will it?' Meaning, if I can't do it quickly, then I'm not that good. I'm not afraid of losing potential clients. They stop being potential clients the moment they want me to work for free. Then they just waste my time. That's why I also speak my mind when somebody asks me: 'Couldn't you just make a quick birthday card? Needn't be anything special.' I know they don't want to sell my work short when they ask that way, but they forget that I am the expert, and my professional pride is important," Birgitte says.

Birgitte is not afraid to challenge what the clients say. "For example, if a client says I have to do the work so they can see it before they sign an agreement, because 'what if they don't like what I make,' then I ask: 'Are you counting on not liking it?' If they doubt whether they like my work, then I'm not the right one to solve the task for them."

On the whole, Birgitte makes sure all formalities are in order so that she doesn't have to waste her time on unhappy clients who may not pay. "I'm not keen on administrative tasks, but I always remember to send bids and get my contracts signed. It's about looking out for yourself. If you can document that work has been done on the assignment after the bid was accepted, the invoice must be paid. I've taken a client to court and won, but it was only because my documentation was in order."

When You
Hit a Wall

Sometimes you run your head into a brick wall, so it can be nice to know how you move past what may seem as a zero point.

Once I made a move that could have spelled the end for my business. It was brought to my attention that there was a government call for tenders that suited what I was doing and wanted to do, namely to counsel self-employed entrepreneurs on their strengths and weaknesses. I decided to put my other projects on standby and went all in to answer the call for tenders. I'd never before considered looking at calls for tenders, and at first glance, it did look massive and complicated to fill out. There were many rules, many documents and many grey areas. It took a long time to fill in, but I was hopeful, because it matched what I'd done up to that point and my natural optimism made me think it'd be fine. I was enthusiastic and saw it as a fantastic opportunity that had landed right at my doorstep.

After waiting for some time, I finally got an answer. I'd forgotten to fill in one line on the last page of a very long document and had therefore been excluded. One line! I was seriously frustrated. The bottom line was,

I knew it was my own fault, having overlooked that line, but there was no mercy, it was explicitly said in the terms and conditions that they wouldn't accept a document incorrectly filled in, and they meant it. I felt like I'd been kicked in the stomach. How could I have overlooked that line!?! It totally sucked the energy out of me, and I felt sad and drained. I'd put so much else aside, and I didn't have anything in the pipeline that could guarantee me an income in the near future. Quite foolish, now that my husband didn't have a job, either. My brain was spinning, reproaching me for how stupid, naive and irresponsible I was.

Most of all, I wanted to shut myself away. Luckily, the summer holidays were about to begin, so I had some time to distance myself from it, but something had to be done quickly if I wanted my business running again before it was too late. I racked my brain for good advice and self-help techniques. What would I say if one of my clients was in the same situation? Often you can get good help by asking your higher self for advice, when you're stuck and need new approaches. I chose to do three things that helped me move forward:

1. First, I talked to my spiritual mentor, who helped me see new possibilities and regain my faith in myself, which really took a burden off my shoulders.

2. Second, I wrote in my calendar that every week I should speak to at least one person who 'understands' me and could help me keep me enthusiastic until the situation turned around again.

3. Last, but not least, I focused on only using my strengths on activities that were directly related to my original business plan, and which would result in more clients.

Things progressed quickly and I remember a couple months later being at a café with a friend. She was impressed with how quickly I'd turned the situation around and come out on top.

If you're in a similar situation, it's important to speak to someone who can help you move forward; they won't necessarily be able to tell you what to do, but they can lift your spirits and help you regain your faith in yourself and your business. Goal-oriented action creates results, so it's all about bouncing back and moving forward again.

Think Positively

After almost 20 years being self-employed, Pia Nissen Tylak has found her own way of tackling adversity.

"When I'm down in the dumps, I'm aware that I don't have to stay there. It's ok to have the blues, but you don't have to remain in that state permanently. It's a choice, a decision. I want to be a hero, not a victim. A thought that activates fear in the autonomic nervous system gives you tunnel vision and makes you secrete cortisol, which decreases your energy. Just like we can be hit by a negative thought, we can also have the capacity to cultivate good things. The very best thing is to cultivate gratitude. We can't be afraid and grateful at the same time. The lowest energy is depression, the highest energy is love and gratitude, so it's about focusing on that. If I think a negative thought, I immediately think of one that's better to correct it."

Besides having positive thoughts, Pia doesn't for a moment doubt that you must have a vision and a clear set of goals to follow: "It's 100% your strongest thoughts that control you. If you want to succeed with something, you must work on it continuously. A good idea is writing things down. It empties your brain of stressful what if-I-forget-something thoughts and makes room for new thoughts. After that, your subconscious mind helps you reach your goal; 90–95% of what you do is governed by your subconscious, automatic responses and habits. Clear goals help your subconscious find the right path," says Pia. She has a process she follows when she wants to turn her ideas and dreams into reality.

"First, your dream or vision must appear and be clear to you. The dream must come straight from your heart. It mustn't be a good idea from your brain, that looks good on paper, but you feel nothing for. When the dream is totally clear to you, you must only focus on it and on implementing it. Instead of becoming insecure and doubtful, you must let go of the notion that it's you who controls the results, and instead believe that it'll come to you when you work towards it. If you have faith, the flow will come where things happen and you see signs. Opportunities reveal themselves when you have faith and you are in the flow. I've always had faith that things would be fine with the businesses I've started. It has helped me focus on solutions, instead of worrying about possible obstacles and problems."

Studies from the Massachusetts Institute of Technology have shown that you learn more from your successes and from focusing on what works than from focusing on your mistakes and what doesn't work. A well-known example is from a bowling competition, where the teams bowled a whole day and were recorded on video. In the evening, team 1 was shown a summary of both good and bad performances, and they learned from that. The next day, they improved their performance by 30%. In the evening, team 2 only saw a summary of their strikes and learned accordingly. The next day, they improved their performance 100%.

By studying failures, you become an expert in what doesn't work. By studying successes, you become an expert in what works. To your advantage, you can make a habit of learning from your and other people's successes. What may help is to keep a diary where you note your insights.

- In which situations do you succeed?
- What do you do precisely?
- How can you use that daily in your business?

It's like a muscle you can train. The more you practice, the better you become at automatically doing what works for you.

Acceptance and Gratitude

It's easy to get caught up in a spiral of wanting more and more and being dissatisfied with your situation because you see others have advanced further and earn more. You feel frustrated and impatient, and you want results to come more quickly. When it happens, don't forget to acknowledge what you've achieved, rejoice over the fact that you have the courage and the resources to follow your dream, and at the same time create a life where you also have time for your children. You're really amazing to start with, because you have the courage to act upon your dream.

If you accept your situation and rejoice over everything you have, you create an easier life for yourself. The periods when my business had the most progress were when I let go of all negative thoughts and concentrated on my work, when I do what I have to without worrying about the result. If you see others achieving something you also want, use their example instead to motivate and inspire yourself – to show that it's possible. Use your energy to create an efficient business.

Everything else is interference. The more dedicated and concentrated you are, the quicker you'll get results.

When you focus on the negative or allow yourself to be irritated, you don't see the opportunities right in front of you because your attention is in the wrong place. A simple, but effective, maxim is to accept your current situation and the things beyond your control, and use your energy to change the things you can influence yourself. Otherwise, you can waste a lot of time thinking and worrying. Like a wise woman once said: "Sometimes you think so much, you find problems that weren't there to begin with."

What the Future Brings

Part of our human need to thrive is being able to contribute and develop ourselves. The journey of being self-employed, with its challenges and successes, goes on even when you reach the first set of goals you have set. New dreams appear and your courage and strength are needed to turn them into reality. An element I found common to all the women I've interviewed is that the dream still lives on, and they're working towards new exciting goals.

Pia Nissen Tylak would like to go abroad with her girls – preferably to California for a year. She'll use her international network, write books and go on stage to inspire more people to get the life they want by listening to their heart, intuition and using their spirituality to guide them.

Birgitte Othel wishes to continue working for her clients and find new tasks for some years. She still has lots to give and wishes to inspire the coming generations of multimedia designers and teach more in the various study programs.

Birgitte Feldborg wants to continue what she's doing, earn more money and retire with her husband in ten years' time, while Pernille Birkenfeldt is enjoying her maternity leave and is ready to get her business moving again come fall.

Jane Ulsøe and her sister, Nanna, are working on marketing Canvas Planner actively in Denmark, and later on in the English-speaking part of the world. They already have users in 30 countries, and their first clients in Sweden. When they have a larger cash flow, they'd like to hire, so they have development, marketing and more customer service in-house.

Anna Bogdanova has big plans, and says, "The challenge of the next five years is to get 'Irresistible', which is a large format, conveyed so we can explain the value of the course, how it functions, and what difference it makes having so much advice along the way."

Louise Ertman Baunsgaard is in the process of defining her new role after selling Letz Sushi. She says "In the end I was ready to do something different and in the last year before selling my share I stepped down as CEO and became the chairman of the board. It felt right to sell and become a mentor and active investor in start-ups. Now, I have invested in four start-ups and am actively involved in two of them."

Camilla Mengers also wants to have more time for her children, and one of her next steps will be to hire help for Albi's Kaffebar so that can become possible.

Anja Lytzen has already come far with Lirum Larum Leg, and even if the business continues growing, time with the family still has top priority. "For me, the goal is having a sensible business and at the same time have time for my children. I think we're in a good place now, with freedom for the children. The trick is maintaining our position and keeping up with the world and the competition."

Louise Ferslev takes everyday life one day at a time, even though she has big dreams for MyMonii. "The vision, and the big desire, is becoming a bank for families with children under the age of 15, totally managed by the parents.

I want to build the business up so it becomes interesting for the big players who may one day want to buy it."

As for me, a big dream has long been writing this book, which is a milestone in my work. I wish to get out and inspire even more mothers to succeed as self-employed entrepreneurs.

As you have read, there are many ups and downs for all self-employed people, but it's a journey filled with freedom and opportunities that provides a quality of life that none of those I've spoken to wish to swap. I hope you delve into the different stories and find new meaning and inspiration as your business develops. There are many women who have gone before you who'd like to share their experiences, so don't be afraid to ask for help or for good advice.

The learning and the knowledge you get from your 'mis-takes' and successes will equip you to have more success with your next attempt. It's not about getting everything right from the start, but adjusting and improving as you go along, and keeping at it until you're where you want to be. You can never know beforehand how things will go, but if you follow your heart and your intuition, and include yourself in your decision-making process, it can never go entirely wrong, because you can still look your-self in the mirror afterwards and know you have been true to yourself.

An Introduction to Christine Gouchault

CHRISTINE GOUCHAULT is a mother of four and business owner. With her company, Mors Business, she has created a community for self-employed women in Denmark with more than 400 members. Through counselling, workshops and lectures, she helps newly started businesses find their place in the market.

Christine has previously had her own recruitment agency in Paris and has 13 years of experience within human resources, sales and marketing. She holds a master's degree in communication and advertisement from INSEEC Paris. In addition to this she is a certified master, business and life coach, and volunteers as a mentor to the entrepreneur students at Copenhagen Business School.

25 TH LID ANNIVERSARY

Sharing knowledge since 1993

- 1993 Madrid
- 2008 Mexico DF and Monterrey
- 2010 London
- 2011 New York and Buenos Aires
- 2012 Bogotá
- 2014 Shanghai